T

Copyright © Greg M

Initial image courtesy of Elle
other images are the ;

Greg McEvoy has asserted his right to be identified
as the author of this Work in accordance with the
Copyrighter, Designs and Patents Act 1988.

First edition 2021. This edition 2024

No part of this publication may be reproduced,
stored in or introduced into a retrieval system,
transmitted, in any form, or by any means (electronic,
mechanical, photocopying, recording, or otherwise),
without the prior permission of the author

EVERYTHING YOU ARE ABOUT TO READ IS TRUE....

THE DYNAMIC DUO IN THEIR YOUTH...

Greg

Steven

**Butter wouldn't melt.....
who knew what came next....?**

FORWARD

True friendship, one that which lasts 30 years or more, is something special. Yes, there has to be a connection, common interests and, as I have found, shared values, work ethic and sense of humour. But, just as importantly, it is also about tolerance and understanding one another's foibles. Everyone has faults, so ignore them. I certainly know what mine are - but that's me. So, my advice is always focus on the positive things that binds a friendship and ensure that you laugh along the way.

Some of the stories and events in this book have been shared with family and friends, usually at social gatherings and usually resulting in a laugh...and often disbelief! During one such occasion in January 2020 I was urged to put pen to paper, if only to capture for the future family generations. For some reason I accepted the challenge – maybe it made sense to capture our exploits for posterity and before we *slip the surly bonds of earth*. I liked the thought of capturing the adventures of two ordinary lads daft adventures in the 1980's and 1990's and 2000's.

I like to think of there is a sense of innocence in what we got up to, perhaps we were the modern-day Huckleberry Fin? I'm sure up and down the country there were other boys with similar tales to tell. There's certainly an Only Fools & Horses feel to some of our escapades and Steve's parents always referred to us as 'The Likely Lads'! We never had any issues with the law, nor gotten into fights, nor committed vandalism or crime. We both had respectable upbringings and were disciplined.... and whilst we were always up for a laugh and pushed the boundaries, we knew where the line was.

Thanks, Steve, for 40 years of mayhem and laughs. Couldn't have written this without your input! Well....I could but I doubt folk would have read it!

Never a dull moment.........and always a tale to tell......

GLOSSARY FOR STEVE..ISM'S
[Expression or Saying = Translation / The Reality]

Trust Me I'm Your Best Mate
- He's looking out for your best interests
- He's looking out for his own best interests

She's Minging
- The girl in question is ugly
- Steve is secretly jealous

I'm Hank Marvin
- I'm starving hungry
- He's going to order everything on the menu and spend a fortune

I'm Brassic
- Got no Money
- I'm not sure I can afford to go out..but we will!

Alright stumpy
- Hello Greg
- Term of endearment

What you doing tonight?
- Steve's throwing a party
- He's already spent £500 before inviting anyone

I'm really into fashion
- He's no idea about fashion
- He's just spent £500 on rubbish fashion

I'm really into sport
- He's no idea about sport
- He's just spent £500 on sports equipment

I've had an idea!
- He's been up all-night cooking up an idea
- Steve's got an unbelievably stupid idea

Sweet Jesus' mother of Mary
- Something strange about this
- Steve's curiosity will get the better of him

I'm Bladdered
- I'm Drunk
- Steve's going to be ill for 2days

I've got a big surprise lined up
- Somebody's going to get humiliated
- Steve will get a belly laugh at someone else's expense A Pleasant

Pheasant Plucker
- A tongue Twister used by Steve when drunk
- He's going to swear in front of the kids again & get away with it...

Diddly Squat
- Sum of nothing
- Worth nought

Big Time
- There's a Problem
- It's Really Bad

Blagging It
- Chancing it / telling a porky
- Standard practice in the Steve book of life!

CONTENT

The 1980s

Chapter 1	In the Beginning
Chapter 2	See You on The Other Side
Chapter 3	Girlfriend Sabotage

The 1990s

Chapter 4	Drink Till Ye Drop
Chapter 5	The Bits Wainwright Missed Day I
Chapter 6	The Bits Wainwright Missed Day II
Chapter 7	Head Banger
Chapter 8	Westmorland Avenue Firework Display
Chapter 9	Trust Me…I'm Your Best Mate
Chapter 10	Male Models
Chapter 11	Put Me Down for a 3-Ball
Chapter 12	The Eagle has Collided

The 2000s

Chapter 13	I'm his Best Mate…Doctor!
Chapter 14	Trust Me…I'm Your Best Man
Chapter 15	Are You Hungry?
Chapter 16	Gone Dutch **Bonus Chapter**

CHAPTER 1 – IN THE BEGINNING
Cheap Trick – Mighty Wings

There is exactly two years and two months age gap between Steve and myself. I had started in the Air Training Corps (ATC) 2501 Squadron, located in Thornton-Cleveleys Lancashire, at the age of 13 and thus when Steve joined the Squadron I was well ensconced in the organisation and had already reached the dizzy heights of Corporal! For those that perhaps aren't aware, the Air Training Corps is a British volunteer-military youth organisation, sponsored by the UK Ministry of Defence and the Royal Air Force; there were several Squadron's located in our area of the North West of England alone. It is a fantastic organisation, teaching self-discipline and various other life skills and played a huge part in shaping me as an individual during my teenage years.

At the point Steve joined I'd already been away on a summer camp to RAF Church Fenton in Yorkshire and another planned for RAF Coltishall in Norfolk. I played drums in the Squadron's Band, participated in military style night exercises, attained marksman level at shooting and undertaken a lot of flying in Chipmunk and Glider aircraft at RAF Woodvale in Southport and British Aerospace Samlesbury. The whole caboodle. Tom Cruise eat your heart out! I was also VERY particular. Some might say OCD, still am to a degree. My shirts and trousers were ironed and pressed to perfection, boots polished to look like glass and beret worn immaculately. I was going places in the Squadron and harboured desires of joining the Royal Air Force. Everything was in check and there was order and semblance in the world.

Then, in 1986, the Squadron brought in a new bunch of oinks, a rather disparaging term for raw recruits. The adult Officers and Non-Commissioned Officers (NCO's) that ran the outfit had clearly been on a recruitment drive at the local schools. Now it was down to the likes of myself to lick this rabble into some shape. Having already been kitted out during an induction session a week earlier the oinks were now turned out for the first time in their 'hand-me-down' uniforms.

One of them in particular looked rather scruffy, with his hair sticking out sideways from under his beret and trousers half-mast. His name was Steve and he seemed to think he was some sort of comedian. From my lofty position as Corporal, he was akin to pond life and should have felt fortunate when I took the time and effort to speak to him. This clown seemed to think he was funny, always cracking the jokes and wooing the girls. Looking back, I do wonder how we struck up an accord?

However, despite the scruffy appearance and other shortcomings I set about turning this particular oink into a suitably attired and well-trained Air Cadet! Indeed, the first thing I did was lend him a comb to sort his hair out, which I hasten to add was never returned! As time passed by, I realised that Steve was a pretty decent lad who, whilst always up for a laugh, was also prepared to get stuck into the square bashing – that's marching up and down to the uneducated – and eventually he turned out well in his uniform. Indeed, unlike myself, Steve went on to join the Royal Air Force but more of that later.

The weeks and months soon passed by and the school summer holiday of 1987 lay ahead, promising 6 hot lazy weeks off school. Whilst I had a week-long summer camp to RAF Coltishall smack in the middle, there were only 2 of us from our Squadron due to attend. I had no other plans for the summer and the initial 3-weeks were free to do what I liked. I had some good pals that lived nearby but I have a recollection of at least one of those pals going off on holiday to Cornwall and another to the Lake District. Whilst my own family did take holidays either in the UK or occasionally abroad, it wasn't every year. Times were much tougher even in the 1980's, unlike today where people can jump on a budget flight on a whim and be in a foreign destination, cheaper than the taxi ride to the Airport! At the time, I definitely recall thinking *I've nobody to hang around with for the next couple of weeks* and, whilst at ATC in the week leading up to the summer holidays, I asked Steve what he was up to the week after and if he fancied hanging out? It was probably a bit random and Steve's reaction said as much, '*oh, err, ok*'. In other words, 'that's a bit strange'. I could have asked any number of pals at the ATC but, for some inexplicable reason, I asked Steve.

It turned out he didn't even live nearby either, and a round cycling trip of 8 miles was needed from Blackpool up to Cleveleys and back. We went to different schools and, apart from a few hours mid-week at ATC, we didn't really know anything of one another. Addresses were exchanged and I agreed to cycle up to Steve's house in Cleveleys. I definitely had a feeling Steve's view was 'I'll be buggered if I'm cycling down to Blackpool'.

The day in question arrived and I recall my mum telling me to take care and stick to the pavements as I set off on my Raleigh BMX bicycle. I recall the back tyre was yellow having randomly been replaced – the front tyre being black. Strange, but again money was tighter back in those days. I made good progress and found Steve's House without any problems. It was a normal semi-detached house and I recall it being very spick-and-span. Steve's Mum and Dad were both at work, his mum a dinner lady at the local primary school that had yet to finish for the summer holidays and his dad working at the local ICI Chemical Plant. I recall his nan called us what seemed to be 12 times per hour throughout the day, to check on us and discuss umpteen other matters, which I found mighty strange. A tour of his abode was completed and record music collection inspected. This confirmed that there was a shared appetite for Rock Music. Bon Jovi no less! Bingo. We had a common interest, which lasts until the current day.

Things were going well, better than expected from both of our perspectives, although I reserved judgement on the REO Speedwagon LP until I'd completed some further research into them! I'd also clocked the framed Lamborghini Countach poster pictures, obligatory in most young lads' bedrooms in the 1980's!

The only area of concern was Steve's choice of bed cushions, Sam Fox printed on them no less (and it must have been cold when they took those photos). Even his two Goldfish were called Sam and Fox? My thoughts were *this is bizarre* but it was as normal as drinking a glass of tap water to Steve.

After a relatively short period of time Steve asked if I was hungry and proclaimed that the local Chippy had just opened? It was well before 12noon and this all felt rather radical and highly unusual for someone with OCD like myself. Up until this point I don't even think I'd ever been to a Chippy on my own before without an adult? Clearly a very sheltered life I had lived thus far. As it happened, the Chippy was literally across the road so off we trundled.

I ordered myself a Chip Barm (Chip butty), which Steve kindly bought for me. He then ordered large Chips, Pudding, Sausage, Fishcake, Barm, curry sauce, gravy, tomato sauce pod, and a litre of coke. I asked Steve '*who else was joining us*' to which he replied 'no one', he was just hungry and, as I was to find out, he has a real problem <u>not</u> ordering everything on the menu when he goes anywhere near a Takeaway or Restaurant! This has been a lifelong illness. He has a complete inability to order a sensible meal that meets one's calorific dietary requirements for one sitting. In the years ahead I have seen an entire KFC menu get ordered in one go. I have seen Chinese Banquets ordered at 1am in the morning and, the daddy of them all, was the entire Sushi menu getting ordered in Disney Springs, Orlando. This boy does NOT know how to hold back and his eyes are definitely much, much bigger than his belly!

After his rather huge and ridiculous lunch we passed the time by taking a tour of the local area before returning to his house to listen to more Rock music. Around 3:30pm the front door could be heard opening. It was his younger brother Neil returning home from School along with their mum Val, who seemed really nice. His brother being home seemed to give Steve a real focus of interest and something destructive to do. I'm not sure what Neil did wrong but only moments after putting his head around Steve's bedroom door to say hello and comment on the loud rock music, I'm pretty sure Steve tormented him about his ginger crop in retaliation, a kerfuffle broke out and Neil found his head getting rammed down the toilet. Cue mum intervention and threats of '*wait until your father gets home*' from downstairs. A standard threat from mothers with unruly kids back in the day!

I realised this was my cue to leave and thus bid my farewell. I don't recall either of us saying, 'we must do this again', but there must have been an affinity of sorts because our friendship went from strength to strength after this *first get-together*.

My own mum was pleased to see me home safely and asked how it had gone? For fear of being banned going back, my reply was 'good, pretty quiet really, just listened to music'. The excessive lunch, loud rock music, saucy bedding material and toilet washing of his brother presented enough intrigue to return, but for me to keep the facts to myself. Having been raised as a Roman Catholic, going to Church every Sunday and attending St. Mary's High School, a former Convent, I wasn't sure whether I needed to tell Sister Maureen about that Sam Fox cushion for fear of being sent for confession!

CHAPTER 2 – SEE YOU ON THE OTHER SIDE
Def Leppard – Animal

One of my earliest and fondest memories with Steve concerned an adventurous day out on our push bikes, which was not long after we'd started to hangout as pals. It was during the summer of 1987. It was also the first proper scrape we'd gotten into and set the tone for the next 35 years!

It was the school summer holidays and, during conversation with Steve a few days prior, he had asked if I was up for a bike ride for the day!? 'Fetch a rucksack each and take some food and drink and go for a long bike ride' he'd said. It sounded like a great idea and a proper little adventure. A modern-day Huckleberry Finn escapade that Mark Twain would approve of. Whilst up for it, I was still a little nervous and wary. I'd played out for the day often enough with my other pals and had my bike with me all day. But I hadn't ventured too far geographically, maybe a few miles tops. I wondered just how far Steve had in mind? As per usual, the dynamic duo had no clear plan, just a concept. However, we had agreed that we might decide on the day where we might go.

The day in question arrived. I woke up and looked out of the window over the back garden where I lived on Warbreck Hill Road, North Shore Blackpool. It was glorious already and clear that a balmy day lay ahead. I sat up and, from my single bed, lifted the window lever and pushed it open to allow the fresh new morn in. I breathed in a lungful of that fresh seaside air some folk travel far and wide to benefit from. I studied the garden scene before me. It wasn't the world's largest garden but of a fair size, neat and compact, with a winding path around the perimeter that my dad had built not long after moving in around 1980. The leaves on the 3 mature Sycamore Trees at the back of the garden were perfectly still, not a breath of wind. Sparrows flitted from branch to branch in some kind of synchronised dance. Small creatures they may have been, but their calls to one another along with the Blackbirds, Thrush and Starlings drifted in through the open window in one cacophony of noise.

The Gulls could not be heard, indicating to me that the tide was out. The garden was in full bloom and looked majestic. It was peaceful and I sat there momentarily pondering the day ahead. It was, looking back, one of those treasured days off school right in the middle of the summer holidays. I hadn't a care in the world. The best days of your life for sure.

It was around 08:30 in the morning but it was already warm and clear it was going to be a hot one. Steve and myself had certainly picked the right day for our cycling adventure!

I got myself washed, dressed and then found a school rucksack that belonged to my brother, made my way downstairs and put some food and a drink bottle containing water inside it. Interestingly enough, 30 years later and I still have that rucksack somewhere …..sorry brother! I don't recall what I took food wise, but our cupboards were never bursting with treats, so it wouldn't have been much. Money was tight and, in any event, my parents were quite strict on what my own children nowadays refer to as 'goodies' e.g. mini-chocolate bars, crisps and such like snacks. They also forbid fizzy drinks. I recall drinking Coca-Cola from a glass bottle in 1977 whilst on holiday in Tunisia as a small boy and thinking how amazing it was! The next time I had it was around 10-

years later as another pal of mine used to have 'the pop man' round once a fortnight. Milkman in the morning, Pop-man at night! Looking back, I feel that my parents made the right decision. I certainly didn't feel like I was missing out. On the subject of money, I had only 20p in my pocket. That was standard operating procedure for kids in the 1980's, it was just enough money to make an emergency phone call home from a public telephone box. Failing that there was always the option of reversing the charges......I doubt the youth of today have a clue what that even means! Can you still reverse the charges? Who knows?

Having checked my white Raleigh BMX over (still with one black tyre and one yellow) I went to give my mum a kiss and tell her what we were up to. 'I'm off to Steve's mum. We're going out for a full day's ride on our bikes'. 'Oh. Where are you going.....don't be going too far', said my mum with genuine concern. 'I'm not sure yet. We're going to decide when I get to his house', 'well don't go too far and keep away from the main busy roads. Do you have some money in case you need to contact us'?, asked my mum. 'Yes, I've got 20p in my pocket and I've got some food. Steve's doing the same'. 'OK son, be very careful. I've got Steve's home number should I need you'.

And with that we bade farewell and I left my mum along with my younger brother Aidan, and 2 sisters Lisa and Fiona, to do their own thing on this glorious day. My dad, on the other hand, was destined for work and his desk at the Civil Service offices on Warbreck Hill Road awaited him!

There were 4 miles I needed to ride to Steve's house. On such a glorious day it was a no-brainer to take the direct promenade route. However, when the weather was a little bleaker, which it often was, I came inland half a mile and took Devonshire

Road. However, today I cycled down to Gynn Square on the promenade, which isn't square and indeed has a rather huge roundabout. It has a large Pub of the same name on the south side of the roundabout but at the turn of the previous century the Pub had been located on the north side along with some small fishermen's cottages. Nothing survives it's *best before date* in Blackpool, once beyond it's economical / useful purpose the bulldozer's come out.....or the occasional mysterious fire!

The ride north along the promenade was an absolute joy. The morning still and fresh, the visibility out to sea superb, there was no wake, the sea being like a millpond. I cycled past the Cliffs Hotel and Castle Casino and on past the Miners Convalescence Home, which stood in its own grounds like a stately mansion. Some of the old boys [Miners] were already sat outside on the benches at the front of the home no doubt enjoying the crystal-clear views across Morecambe Bay towards Barrow and, tracing slightly to the east of Barrow the English Lake District Mountains. So clear they were that it felt I could cycle there is no time but the reality was that the Lake District was a good hour away by car! It always surprised me how well turned out the old Miners were – shirt, tie and blazers. Very dapper. I like it when old people make the effort to look after their appearance. On I rode past Bispham and down towards the iconic Norbreck Castle Hotel, which looks today exactly as it did 35 years ago. This huge monolithic looking building, whose ramparts gave it the appearance of a Castle, was actually built as a large private country house in 1869. Some house....as a hotel it currently has 480 bedrooms! Finally, I drew nearer to Cleveleys and cycled past the pitch-and-putt course on the promenade, one of the best I've ever played on but sadly now gone.

I used to love going on that par 3 course with my brother and family. I rode on past Victoria Road West with its little funfair on the promenade, although it was too early for any trade but no doubt the proprietor would do well on such a day. Finally, I reached The Royal Hotel and Pub (in more recent years changed to The Venue) maybe half a mile north of Victoria Road West. It was another large establishment and once used as Polish Hospital during the 2nd World War.

I took a right turn onto Carlin Gate [street] and then on towards Fleetwood Road where I took a left before taking a 2nd right onto Westmorland Avenue where Steve and his family lived. I parked my bike up under the bay window and rapped the glass on the door window, there being no doorbell. 'Come on round here' shouted Steve, who was somewhere down the side of the house near the garden. Sure enough I found Steve round the back with a brand-new gleaming Mountain Bike. I should add that Mountain Bikes were *new* and very much replacing the BMX as the preferred mode of transport for youths. I was both impressed and a tad jealous, my own wheels looking rather forlorn in comparison. 'Nice Bike Steve', I had to give it to him. 'Early birthday present, good eh!'. Blimey, 3 months early no less!' I said a little surprised, his birthday being early October. 'So, where we going Steve' I asked, hoping that it wouldn't be anything too daring'. 'Well, I thought we could go across the Shard Bridge, go over Wyre and explore. What say you McAttack'. I was a little unsure. Some of the roads out of Cleveleys, in particular the A585 Amounderness Way, were like racing tracks and carried huge articulated lorries coming away from the Fleetwood Docks. 'I don't know. I think that could be a little dangerous Steve. The main road is really busy'. Steve looked at me with a degree of understanding, 'it is, but it's after rush hour so will be quieter. And besides, we can stick to the paths as much as possible until we cross the River Wyre Shard Bridge, which also has a path. It's much quieter too once you get to Hambleton'. I thought on it momentarily, something that became the norm over the next 35 years! 'Ok. Let's be really careful though' I said. Steve smiled pleased that I'd been won over. 'Where are we going to go once we get other there' I asked? 'Dunno, there are loads of fishing ponds and lakes I can show you, so we know for next time we want to go fishing'. It seemed like a reasonable idea and besides, Steve was right, it would be much quieter once across the river Wyre.

Over Wyre, as it is referred to locally, is an area north of the River Wyre that has a string of villages heading west to the sea, such a Hambleton, Stalmine, Preesall and finally Knott End. I like it Over Wyre, it has a nice feel and is much quieter than Blackpool and its surrounding area. Steve had already stocked up his own rucksack with lots of food and treats. We had enough supplies between us to ensure that we didn't go hungry or thirsty and we were ready to go! It was one of those rare days in the last 35 years that Steve was actually ready to go anywhere early in the morning! We briefly said goodbye to Steve's Mum and set off into the unknown. The scene lives vivid in my memory.

We cycled west, away from Steve's house up Cumberland Avenue and then West Drive towards Thornton. True to his word, we kept to the paths as much as possible. As Steve had predicted, it wasn't that busy now that rush-hour had ended. We passed The Gardeners Pub, a huge old-fashioned building where Steve proclaimed that his mum and dad met, something I never forgot. We kept on going, through Thornton, over the railway line and passed the Bay Horse Pub and on passed the site of the former Illawalla country club venue, which the oldies used to rave about for a night out in the 1970's and 1980's. Eventually we re-joined the exceptionally busy A585, now at Mains Lane. However, there was a decent enough path for us here to stay safe on until we reached the Shard Bridge.

Eventually we reached the Shard Bridge. The bridge was rebuilt in 1993, but at the time of our mini cycling adventure folk were still using the original bridge that had been built in 1864.....and you could tell! It had the appearance of one of Blackpool's piers, with a significant number of cast iron legs and yellow side panels. The road across was incredibly uneven and it had a feeling that it was quite literally on its last legs and unsuitable for modern heavy traffic. Having said that, it had a charm of its own. It connected the Fylde coast with the aforementioned villages and old shipbuilding yards such as Wardleys Creak. I could only imagine the scene 100 years earlier, in its Victorian Heyday. As we cycled across, getting bounced up and down, we both looked either side of the river. The tide was out. Once we reached the other side, we stopped adjacent the Shard Pub, a popular watering hole for those water-skiing and jet skiing. 'I've been here with my uncle water skiing Greg. We should do that sometime', said Steve pointing to where the boats were tied during high water. And jolly nice it looked too. In time, we would both go water-skiing.... but more of that later!

On reaching the village of Hambleton the daytime traffic had really eased off and we could start to relax. I have a fond childhood memory, a flash-back I can still see today, of cycling through Hambleton with the sun on my face, of looking ahead at Steve pedalling away and smiling to myself. Two pals, enjoying one another's company on a treasured summers day, taking in the scenery and having a proper little adventure. I had a feeling deep inside that this day out might cement our friendship, maybe it did. But as we cycled along with not a care in the world little did I know that this blossoming friendship was about to be tested….

Not long through Hambleton and Steve gestured for us to pull over and get off our bikes. We weren't going too fast so stopped fairly quickly, jumped off our bikes and leaned them against an old faded wooden fence, with an open and empty farmers field beyond. 'I've had an idea Greg' said Steve enigmatically, 'let me know what you think'. Hmm….I was suspicious before another word had left his mouth. 'We *could* cycle round some of the country lanes like we said we would, you know looking for ponds to fish, and go back the way we came, *or* we could cycle down to Knott End and see if the Ferry is running across to Fleetwood? That will save us cycling all the way back the way we came'. 'I'm not so sure about that Steve', I said with growing concern. 'Well, I'm not even sure if it's running, but if it is it would save us one heck of a journey back. It would probably save more than half our journey and, besides that, my Nan and Grandad live on the other side in Fleetwood. We could pop round, use their toilet and get a drink. They wouldn't mind. So, why don't we just cycle on and see'? The blighter! I was damn sure he'd hatched this one the night before but kept it from me until we were well into the journey. I also wasn't convinced this was such a good idea, 'how far is it from here to the Ferry point at Knott End and how much is the Ferry'? I asked Steve with furrowed brow. Steve, as per usual was much more relaxed about the state of affairs, 'it's not far, maybe only 2 or 3 miles and I'm pretty sure the Ferry will be running on a day like today. If not then we just come back the way we came', 'how much is it? I replied, 'it's only about 15p and I've got about 40p anyway' said Steve in a calm manner. I paused for thought, 'go on then, let's go'. And with that we got back on our bikes, this time with a chocolate bar to munch on route, courtesy of Steve. Maybe it was the sweetener?

On and on we rode…..and on and on. Whilst I know now that it wasn't that far, for 2 young teenagers it did feel *much* further that Steve had led me to believe. No surprise there then! We cycled on through Stalmine, down the hill past the Old Black Bull Pub at Preesall and then on towards Knott End. I'd driven through Knott End fairly often when helping out at the nearby sailing club, but I hadn't cycled through the village before and it certainly gave me a different perspective. It had and still does have a charm of its own. There were lots of independent shops, Butchers, Florists, Newsagents etc and I suspected everyone knew everyone. The demographic was definitely in the plus 60 region and 2 young lads cycling down the high street brought that average down a tad! Finally, we reached the promenade that had a long row of Victorian terrace housing facing out over the stunning expanse of Morecambe Bay, all 192 square miles of it!

The old faces at the windows of the immaculately kept Victorian properties gazed at us and beyond, maybe thinking on their own youth and friends now departed. It was a far cry from the rammed promenade in Blackpool, whose famous Tower could be seen way in the distance. For there today it would be absolutely rammed with Tourists, families spending their hard-earned cash on the roller coaster and donkey rides and in doing so making their own memories to look back on in years to come.

Eventually we reached the esplanade that led down to the Ferry, 'look Greg!'; shouted Steve still peddling away, 'the Ferry is running!' he shouted with great delight. Indeed, the bright red Ferry was chugging through the water across the short distance to Fleetwood on the other side of the River Wyre. I say short distance, but this was the river estuary, going out into the Irish sea, and it was much, much wider there than it was further back at the Shard Bridge. Indeed, the P&O cargo Ferries still ran from Fleetwood to Ireland and the estuary was dredged often to maintain that service.

Eventually we stopped and got off our bikes to admire the view and take in some water on what had become a very warm day. The river was a hive of activity, the tide now having well and truly turned. There were small Toppers and Lasers from the nearby sailing club scooting around being overseen by a couple of safety ribs, the od larger sailing yacht and people on the Fleetwood side of the river down on the beach in the distance. I could clearly see the North Euston Hotel. A majestic curved Victorian Hotel that had a prime view across the river and out over Morecambe Bay. 'Right, let's go and get a ticket for the next crossing said Steve' and with that we walked our bikes down to the small ticket booth, where a rather grumpy middle-aged individual awaited us. 'Can we have 2 single Tickets to Fleetwood Please' said Steve with me stood behind him, 'that'll be £1.10'. The colour drained from my cheeks, '£1.10. No. We just want to go one way' said Steve now with a little panic in his voice'. 'Sorry lads, its 55p each and that's it and I'm not charging you for your bikes either, so I'm doing you a favour'. 'Err. Ok.' Said Steve, like someone who'd just been checkmated. My chin was on the floor. Now we had to cycle all the way back. Much further than we'd planned and furthermore I had the added joy of another 5-miles on top of what Steve had to do to get home to North Shore Blackpool!!

Steve pulled me away from the ticket booth. 'I've had an idea', 'oh please save me O'Lord.....not another one....look at the mess we're in now. You and your flipping ideas'. Steve chuckled, 'hang on stroppy knickers. We'll be fine. Let me get the Ferry to Fleetwood as we've enough money for 1 Ticket. I can then cycle to my Nan's and get some more money for your ticket. I'll then cycle back to the beach on the other side and, when you see me waving both my hands above my head like this it will be your cue to jump on board the Ferry. You see.....I'll have the money waiting on the other side'. I winced at such a stupid idea and felt the day had taken a turn for the worse, 'are you bonkers?! Is your Nan in? Do you know for sure she'll be there? And will she give you the money' I said sternly. 'Well, she'd definitely give me the money but I'm not sure if she's in'. 'Why don't you call her to check' I said not really thinking that one over, 'because we've only 60p between us and then we'd both be cycling back no matter what', 'oh yeah', I said. 'But I'd be stuck here on my own if she's not in'. Steve's mind was thinking through the alternative, 'well my mum is definitely in, so I'd just cycle to Cleveleys if my Nan is out and then cycle back to Fleetwood with the money'. My furrowed brow deepened, 'but that's about a 4mile round trip.....you might be gone for ages'. Steve was adamant, 'look, even if my Nan is out my Grandad will be in. He's not so well so doesn't go out so much.

We'll be fine. Trust me I'm your best mate'. How could I argue with that? 'Go on then but jump up and down and wave both arms if it's safe to come over. If not just wave your left arm and then I'll have to cycle all the way home on my own'. Looking back, it was a hair-brain idea. The day was already marching on and I worried as to how long Steve might be gone. I was still young and miles from home on the wrong side of a fast-flowing river. Steve could see my concern and unhappiness with the situation, 'Don't worry. I'm not going to leave you here. I'll sort it'. I nodded without saying a word. And with that Steve walked off to the ticket booth pushing his bike along beside him.

By this point the small red Ferry had returned and was in the process of unloading its latest cargo of fare paying passengers. It wasn't a big boat and probably only held 20 passengers at a time. It was small and resembled a bright red tug boat. The tide was coming in at a pace and the unloading point was also already much further up the slipway that led down to the river. I watched Steve walk down to join a number of other passengers, maybe only 6 or 7 of them in total. It made me angry, I could quite easily have been on that boat. Looking back, I do wonder if the man might have been more reasonable if he'd only known our predicament. I suspect he might have shown leniency!

Eventually it was Steve's turn and in he climbed, the two Ferrymen loading his bike in separately once all persons were aboard. The ropes were undone from their tie points and the ferry instantly drifted with the tide away from the slip road. It's engines revved up and it quickly rotated almost on the spot to face it's return leg to Fleetwood. The crossing was short, maybe only 10 minutes but all of a sudden, I started to feel incredibly lonely. Like I'd been left stranded in some warped disaster movie.

There were people around me walking in the beautiful sunshine eating ice-creams and being harassed for any scraps by the Gulls that were now returning from the eating fest out on the Morecambe Bay flats for their desserts! But I could take no notice of what was going on around me. I was transfixed on the little red ferry that was slowly diminishing in size. Eventually it reached the other side.

It was only then that it occurred to me just how small people looked on the other side. They were just dots, undistinguishable. And whilst I strained to see Steve I could not…..I looked for someone with a bicycle but for the love of trying I could see nothing.

I was sure that Steve had been unloaded and was on his way but I had seen nobody that looked remotely like Steve. I decided not to think on it too much and that he would be back in next to no time, Steve had explained that his Nan lived relatively near to the Ferry port and that he shouldn't be more than 10 or 15 minutes…. maybe 20 minutes max once on the other side.

I waited. I started to relax a little and take in my surroundings a bit more. Off to my left in the distance was a small row of former fishermen's cottages, now owned by Lancashire County Council and used as a sailing venue for schools across the County. I knew this as I helped out there occasionally; I was quite familiar at sailing these waters. Turning 180 degrees I could see the Knott End Golf Club, which ran alongside the river and across the carpark was a Cafeteria and pivoting round further the Bourne Arms Pub. There were plenty of people around but I felt isolated and worried about my predicament.

I decided to walk down to the slip road, to be nearer the river so I could see across to the pebble beach on the Fleetwood side. The people on the beach in Fleetwood looked like dots. We were 10 minutes now so I started scanning the horizon.

People just looked like matchsticks out of a Lowry painting. They were people alright but there was nothing distinguishable about them. Steve had been wearing a white T-Shirt but, you guessed it, the swathes of people on that far shore seemed to be wearing white, no doubt owing to it being a hot sunny day. I waited and waited….it became interminable. My frustration grew and grew. I kept scanning the horizon, every dot moving on that beach but I could not see Steve. I cursed him thinking that maybe he had returned but left his bike at his Nan's, for surely, I would have seen a boy with a bike on the other side? Or was his Nan and Grandad out and Steve now peddling furiously for Cleveleys? God forbid!

I waited for another 15 maybe 20 minutes, all told around 50 minutes, pushing towards the hour mark. The afternoon was heading towards evening and I started to think about my family, about them worrying where I was. I panicked about cycling home in poor light amongst the rush hour traffic and getting knocked over. I was done. I couldn't wait anymore. I had to make a decision now to either cycle home or chance it on the boat. I decided on the latter.

The Ferry boat was on its way back to Knott End. I therefore decided to chance it and seek sympathy from the Ferrymen rather than the miserable ticket master. I walked past the ticket booth and made my way down to the slipway. The tide was much, much higher now so the Ferry came further up the slipway. I queued up with 2 or 3 other people, there weren't too many for this journey. When it came to my turn one of the Ferrymen helped me over the side given the boat was bobbling around a little. As with Steve, my bicycle was loaded in last and the men cast off. Before I knew it, the boat was cast free and engines roaring away and we turned majestically in the incoming tide and started to head towards Fleetwood. Whilst one Ferryman steered the boat the other came round to collect the tickets. He came for my ticket last having collected from the other customers first. Just as well as we were about a third of the way across already. The Ferrymen held out his hand, 'ticket please'. I gave it puppy dog eyes, 'I have no ticket. My pal is waiting on the other side with some money for me'. The Ferryman looked like he hadn't encountered this scenario before, 'you've got no ticket?' he said incredulously. 'No. I didn't have enough money so my pal came across to get some money from his Nan. He will be there I promise'. I had no idea if Steve would be there or not! The Ferryman smiled, 'well, he better be, otherwise I think we'll have your bike'. At the time I took this as read.....if Steve wasn't there I was going to be handing over my bike. But now, as an adult, I think I can see that he was jesting and I would have been allowed on my way. I sat in silence, fretting and cursing Steve, my neck strained to scan every nook and cranny of the beach on the other side and the pier docking area where the Ferry would berth. Nothing. I could not see him anywhere and my heart sank.

After a few more minutes the Ferry gingerly manoeuvred into its berth, jostling around against the incoming tide, which seemed to be causing more swell on this side of the river. I stood up peering for Steve and caught the eye of the Ferryman who was looking at me expectantly. And there. All of a sudden, Steve came bounding into view coming down an iron ramp on the pier! 'He's there, he's there' I shouted at the Ferryman who smiled at me as I stood bolt upright, pointing at Steve who was stood maybe 40 – 50 feet away. 'Jolly good, I guess we won't be keeping your bike then after all' he said whilst he coiled a rope ready for throwing ashore to a third hand on the gangway. 'Hallelujah' I shouted at Steve, 'thanks mate, where the hell were you, couldn't see no waving going on near the beach'! I said both in relief and with a degree of sarcasm. 'I've been here for ages, why the hell didn't you come over sooner'. 'Here? You said the beach!!! I've been looking on the beach the whole time and meanwhile you've been hiding in amongst this pier gantry….no wonder I couldn't see you……what a plonker'!! Our public debate drew great amusement from the other fee-paying passengers and crew, *what a right pair we have here* they surely must have thought! Steve paid the Ferryman who helped me get my bike off the boat, smiling all the while. I glanced back at Knott End, now safely in the distance. Phew……I'd made it. I was full of relief. As we walked up the pier gantry that led onto the promenade, there was much jocular behaviour between the two of us, 'I couldn't distinguish between men and women, everyone looks like ants from over there, I cried, 'my flipping arms are hurting I was waving them so much' said Steve. But there were smiles all round, 'come on Greg, let's go and see my Nan and Grandad, they want to see us both', and with that said we jumped on our bikes and rode the short distance to Ash Road in Fleetwood to thank his Nan and Grandad for bailing us out.

I recall this part of the trip as I got to meet Steve's Grandad, Robert, who he often spoke about, including his D-Day landing exploits in a Tank. We, found his Nan's house in no time at all and I had visions of Steve having a nice little rest and chat with his Grandparents before coming back with the money, but he assured me not! The house had an alleyway at the rear where we took our bikes and left them. I then followed Steve into the old but large Victorian terrace house. His Nan, Mary, met us in the hallway and was delighted to see that I'd made it, 'my, my, you have been a long way. What on earth possessed you to ride all the way to Knott End….and with no money'!?

I felt that the question was being directed at me! Better redirect that question, 'Good question Nan' I replied, 'better ask Steve that one'. 'Agh, I see, there was no issue with the men on the boat then', she asked, 'no, they were fine and thank you so much for the money. I'll get it back for you' I said respectfully. 'No, no, don't be stupid. It was only a few pence. Come on through and meet Robert'. We were taken into the back room that joined to the kitchen and there was Steve's Grandad Robert. He clearly wasn't a well man and had a respirator fitted. But we joined him at the table and spent maybe 40-minutes talking about our adventure and the close scrape! I think they were genuinely pleased to see us and listened intently to what we'd been up to. We had a drink and some biscuits and were thoroughly looked after. I could see Steve was very close to his Grandad and hung on every word he said. He seemed like a fantastic man, but sadly that was to be the first and last time I was to see him.

It was well into the afternoon now, where the day had gone I didn't know. We therefore bade our farewells to Steve's Grandparents Mary and Robert, and set off together in the direction of Cleveleys. Steve took the opportunity to show me his High School……I was suitably underwhelmed. It looked like a 1940's throwback. I don't think Steve cared much for the place either. On we went passed Rossall School, which is one of the leading private schools in the country, talk about contrast! After another mile or so we came to Westmorland Avenue and both slowed down. 'Cheers Steve, that was some day out. Best not mention to my mum what happened though'. Steve smiled, 'what happened on the tour stays on the tour. Maybe see you tomorrow buddy', he said and with that turned to peddle the short distance to his front door. I on the other-hand had a further 4 miles to grind out. After a rather long day in the saddle, it felt like hard work and a real chore. I was tired, sticky and hot. I couldn't wait to get home. However, all journeys do indeed come to an end eventually and, after one final long hard slog up the hill from the Gynn I was home.

I put my bike away in the garage at the front and let myself in through the front door, 'hi son, is that you back' shouted my mum from the kitchen. She continued to talk as I entered the kitchen, 'Good timing as I'm just putting the tea on. Glad to see you're safe, where did you go?', she said now looking across the island unit at me, 'Oh, not too far, just up near the river at Stanah' I said thinking *if only she knew*. 'Oh, good. Well go and get yourself cleaned up by which time dinner will be ready'. And with that I trudged upstairs to where my day had started several hours earlier.

CHAPTER 3 – GIRLFRIEND SABOTAGE
Poison – Nothing but a Good Time

During the 1980's Blackpool was still going strong as a tourist destination, although the heady days of the 1960's and 1970's were long gone given the rise in package holidays to places such as Spain. The long weekend had become the staple diet of B&B's and Hotels along the Golden Mile, although this started to drift from the traditional family holiday to the Hen and Stag parties. As a consequence, the rather dated discotheque matured into the Nightclub and Blackpool had an array of venues that were of a very high standard. The jewel in the crown was The Palace Nightclub, and became nationally famous through the very late-night show Hit Man & Her, as presented by Peter Waterman and Michaela Strachan. The Palace Nightclub was famous for its light show. It is hard to describe to anyone reading this, but it was truly awesome and years ahead of its time. I had never seen anything like it at the time nor since! A huge inverted column of lighting descended over the crowd on the dancefloor. It opened up like a blossoming orchid and burst into a Lazer show with Lazer lights bouncing of strategically positioned small mirrors around the club. It was truly incredible.

People stopped to watch it, a highlight of the evening. This Nightclub was one of the best in the UK at the time….no question. It was also massive and could accommodate a few thousand people. I'm sure if you go looking you will find some footage on the Internet.

In the late 1980's the Palace Nightclub cottoned onto the idea of offering up an Under 18's Club experience, much earlier in the evening. Why not. The building was otherwise sat idle, so the business opportunity was realised. It was the real deal for the local teenagers and offered up exactly the same experience that the adults got, except of course there was no alcohol. They even threw in the bouncers, who did a great job at controlling the kids. Of course, there wasn't a chance Steve and myself were going to miss out on this opportunity! In reality, I don't actually remember going that often, maybe half a dozen times at most. I do recall that on one occasion there was a crowd crush when queuing up outside and I was literally lifted off my feet and couldn't breathe. There was plenty of screaming and a pandemonium but fortunately the Bouncers realised what was happening and sorted things out. It was nonetheless a rather frightening experience at the time and I think the saga put us off. However, I digress, as the following story pre-dates this incident.

It was probably only the 2nd or 3rd time that The Palace were holding the U18 Club event and the word was out… *'you've gotta go….it's brilliant*' and so on and so forth. This was a no brainer for Steve and myself, we had to go and check this out. So, on the said Friday evening Steve and myself got kitted out in our best jeans and polo-shirts (no shell suits allowed at The Palace!) and rendezvoused on the Tram, Steve having jumped on at Cleveleys and myself joining him at Gynn Square. In no time at all we were up alongside the world-famous Blackpool Tower and jumped off the tram on the Golden Mile. The Palace Nightclub was at the top of a very wide staircase, which we climbed. There was a throng of noise coming from above and on reaching the last few steps we could clearly see a huge queue of kids along the outer wall of the Nightclub from the main entrance, where 3 or 4 bouncers kept watch prior to opening time. I recall it was a beautiful summers evening. The sun was still reasonably high over the Irish Sea and the promenade was alive with Tourists out for an evening stroll having left their guest houses and hotels. There was a cacophony of noise wafting in from the Coral Island Amusements building adjacent, a mini-Las Vegas. Bright lights, the sound of Arcade games, a bingo caller and the ever-present smell of burgers, hot-dogs and suchlike Tourist fodder.

On walking down the queue to join at the end we recognised a few friendly faces, some from school and others from the Air Training Corps. But there were literally hundreds that we didn't know and there was a real buzz of excitement. We waited patiently and eventually, around 7pm, the doors opened... but it seemed to take an eternity to get to the front doors as people fumbled to pay in their cash and hand coats in at the cloakroom.

I hadn't been in The Palace Nightclub before or indeed any Nightclub and, once inside the building, it was really quite exciting. There was an anti-room with a cloakroom (as mentioned) and ticket booth and then two large double doors that took you into the Club. The music was already thumping and the crowd seemed like a good bunch. I had a feeling that it would be a good night. Eventually we were paid up and ready, 'come on then McAttack.....let's do this' and with that Steve pushed hard against one of the double doors and in we went.

My first impression was wow! This was a glitzy big Club! It was brilliant and the neon lights made Steve's Gola trainers and white T-Shirt glow a brilliant white and indeed my own clobber too.

I thought we looked rather sophisticated under this lighting. I should also add that I was not knocking Steve's Gola trainers.....at least he had a brand! I was on Shoe markets finest unbranded pumps!

Despite the hoard that had been queuing outside, and us being located somewhere near the back, as a collective the crowd barely filled the place. The Palace Nightclub had a capacity of 3,000 Clubbers. That is a lot of people. However, I dare say that only 200 – 300 youths had queued to get in, so my lasting impression was that we'd barely dinted the place in terms of filling it. However, the management hadn't limited access to any particular area. This was good news as the Club had different levels and viewing areas over the main dance floor. It was a labyrinth, an adult's playground for sure, with different bars and dance floors and viewing areas. A fabulous Club with apparently no expense spared on the décor.

Having purchased a drink Steve and myself wandered around for a while and bumped into plenty of other boys whom we knew. We exchanged the usual banter but we didn't stop and talk to them for too long as Steve, as per usual, was more inclined to find some nice ladies to talk to.

I recall we bumped into several girls near the upper dance floor, immediately behind the DJ booth overlooking the main dance floor, which was already full of kids strutting their stuff. I didn't know any of them but Steve knew them all as they went to the same school. There were maybe 6 or 7 of them, so a fair crowd.

The evening then followed the usual pattern with Steve going into banter overdrive and me trying to catch up. I have a recollection of Steve asking if anyone was hungry, nothing ever changes, and disappearing somewhere with 2 or 3 of the girls whom he knew well, possibly to get some hot-dogs and more drinks insisting that I stay put and that he'd be back. So I was left stranded with maybe 3 or 4 unfamiliar female faces. I was never particularly comfortable nor confident talking to the opposite sex. I'd been a proper lads lad, right up to my late teens.... more interested in ATC, camping, air rifles, climbing trees and the like.......clinging onto my youth. I guess like a lot of people I was also afraid of rejection and making a fool of myself, which made me more timid. Steve on the other hand was making Del Boy look like an amateur! How some of the girls fell for his lines I shall never know!

Either way I was mighty surprised when an extremely attractive girl started talking to me. With Steve gone and the accompanying bravado and spin had also gone with him and I found myself just being me. I struck up really good conversation with the young lady in question. She was very attractive but also down to earth and we struck an accord straight away. I couldn't tell you what we chatted away about but probably, school, holidays and personal likes and dislikes etc, but I felt quite comfortable for a change. Things seemed to be going well and, quite remarkably for me at the time, I plucked up the courage and asked if she might like to perhaps go on a date? I was pretty gobsmacked when she said 'yes' and felt like I was on a bit of a roll.

That's when things started to turn. Several feet away and stood with the girls he'd disappeared with to get food and drinks, was Steve. He'd clearly been eyeing up the blossoming romance from a distance. He wandered over and casually asked if he might have a private word away from the lady in question? A little puzzled I pulled myself away from my new date and followed Steve over to a table a few yards away. 'What do you think you're doing with her?', came the question from Steve, 'well, she seems really nice and I've asked her on a date'. There was a look of terror in Steve's eyes, 'Greg (no nickname, so serious) I'm telling you, you do NOT want to go out on a date with her'! I was perplexed, 'well why not, she seems rather nice to me' I replied. Steve then went on a diatribe of reasons not to go on a date, 'wrong side of town, smells, in the wrong crowd, you'll regret it for the rest of your life' and then the one to seal it, 'trust me….I'm your best mate'. Now, at this juncture in my life I guess I'd only known Steve 3 or 4 years and being young, gullible, not particularly confident with the opposite sex yet and easily influenced I took heed of his advice. I thus started to distance myself from the young lady and mingle with the rest of the crowd thereafter. After a while, maybe an hour or so, she came over and asked if we were still going to go on a date (and presumably to exchange contact details etc) but I rather appallingly told her that I'd 'changed my mind'. She took it well given she hadn't long met me. I wasn't sure I'd made the right decision but mates are mates and look out for one another right…..don't they?

The evening soon came to an end. I think the U18's disco only ran for 2hrs and then it was a case of everyone out so the Club could be tidied and made ready for the adults later on. We'd had a great night and great fun but I couldn't help thinking that maybe I should have gone on that date?

Still, we were merely young lads and there were plenty more fish in the sea and years ahead of us. Nothing more was said. So, we grabbed a greasy burger from a promenade vendor and caught the Tram home.

About a fortnight later I was sitting at home on a Friday evening with nothing much to do, Steve and other pals all being unavailable. My Dad called me into the living room and explained that there was an in-shore powerboat race happening on the Blackpool coast the next day and it was being filmed for Sky TV no less! Being a teenager, I initially declined his offer of a family outing [boring!], but this was countered with 'what else on you doing in the morning? Why don't you come along with your Mum, little Sister and myself, you can catch up with Steve later in the day'. He was right, Steve didn't do mornings, especially on a Saturday, so I relented and said I would come. Who knew, I might even enjoy it.

The next morning was stunning. I have always been a morning person, which makes my friendship with Steve's all the more remarkable because he isn't! On a hot summer's morn, as this was, I long for the freshness of the new day. The opportunity to sit in the garden with a nice cup of tea, fresh glass of orange and marmalade on toast. For me it always was and still is the most important part of the day. I just don't understand anyone who misses such stunning mornings. But I digress. Not before too long my dad, mum and little sister ensembled in the hallway ready for the off. The day was already a hot one. One of those rare days on the Fylde Coast that you can count on one hand in a calendar year where it was going to be *cracking the flags*. For those who are not of northern heritage, may I explain - many of the pavements in the area were stone flagged and prone to crack when extremely hot. Which of course in the North West of England is extremely rare! So, when it's *cracking the flags* the thermometer is usually setting local records! The organisers of the in-shore boat race must have been pinching themselves. It was truly glorious weather.

My parents lived (and still live) only a short walk from the Blackpool Promenade in the north shore area. The 4 of us therefore walked down to the promenade in the sunshine.

On reaching the promenade the sea was like a mill pond. No wake whatsoever. And we could see and hear some incredibly powerful and noisy speedboats warming up on practice runs ahead of the big race in a few hours' time. From Gynn Square, at north shore, the promenade has 3 levels; top, middle and lower. We decided to take the middle promenade and walked towards North Pier where we could see far ahead of us crowds of people, the sound of someone speaking over a Tannoy, loud music and lots of flags as you might see at a Grand Prix race. After a 20-minute walk we reached North Pier and it was packed. There were umpteen Super Speedboats on low-loaders being readied to take down the slip way to be lowered into the water, the tide now having turned. Others were on the promenade itself, presumably for races later on. The place was packed and it had an F1 race feel about the place. The tourists were clearly loving it, although for a working man's holiday destination there was some serious wealth on display. Definitely a case of rich man's toys far out of the reach of the average man who came to Blackpool for a holiday weekend.

Nonetheless, we took great interest in the boats on display. My Dad had a small fishing boat at the time, which we regularly went out to sea on. So, we knew the waters here well and took an interest in anything marine. It was at that point that my Mum said, 'Wow....just look at this one Greg'. Indeed, there was one boat that certainly stood out in the crowd. It was the daddy of them all and I can only imagine how much it must have cost. It was gold and white and looked brand knew, with several huge outboard engines located at the rear. It sat proudly on its gleaming low-loader. Even better, it had a stunning blonde resplendent in bikini and sunglasses bathing on it! Surely, I should have told my side-kick Steve about this after all!! He'd have gotten up earlier for sure!

I was lost momentarily gawping at this magnificent powerboat that my Mum had drawn our attention to, when the bathing beauty sat up and lowered her glasses to stare across at me, 'Greg…..Greg…..is that you?' My jaw dropped and I froze. Oh……My…….God………..it was the same girl I had met at The Palace Nightclub only a fortnight earlier and declined to date on the basis that my *best mate* told me to trust him and not to! 'Oh, hi……yes, it's me…..what you doing up there'……feeling rather sheepish at this point as my Mum, Dad and sister moved in around me looking puzzled as to how I know this girl, 'Oh, it's my Dad's. Nice isn't it. He's racing it later on'. 'Yes, it's amazing, you're very lucky' I replied. OK. So, at this point I admit it, I wanted to i) kill Steve and ii) let the ground swallow me up. This was not good news. This girl was beautiful…..and there were clearly zero reasons why I should have listened to Steve. The conversation continued, 'I say, who you with down there?' came the reply. 'Errm, I'm with my Mum and Dad and Sister', 'Aww, that's nice being out with the family, well enjoy your day Greg'. And with that she pushed her shades up with good effect and lay back down to continue sunbathing. There was no 'do you fancy having a look around', or 'are you sure you still don't want to go on that date'? Nope. I was left there stood feeling like a candle in the wind. Completely and deservedly blown out. And as if it couldn't get any worse the proverbial elbow struck my ribcage, 'who's that then Greg' said my Mum, 'errm, just a girl that Steve knows', 'oh she seems really nice'. I didn't need the Spanish Inquisition from the oldies, please can the ground swallow me up ran through my head. 'Yes Mum. Anyway, can we go home now....I've seen enough' came my grumpy reply.

I wanted to get out of there ASAP. I wanted to get on the phone to Redman pronto and explain that he had probably ruined my life. Sure enough, on reaching home in record time, I called Steve's house and made sure that his Mum went to fetch him out of bed. I gave him both barrels, 'you absolute sod Redman…..!' and I explained the mornings events.

Steve was, as always, sympathetic, 'look, I did you a favour, you really need to trust me on this one, besides who needs a powerboat…. and we're going to be millionaires anyway, so you can buy 3 of them if you like. And besides, she wasn't that good looking anyway….if she was she'd have gone out with me'. Boom….and there we had it. Let the truth be known! Girlfriend sabotage!!!

CHAPTER 4 – DRINK TILL YE DROP
The Shamen – Ebeneezer Goode

Not all the stories in this book are necessarily long, including this one which is very much a story of misadventure and points to the dangers of drinking too much. For many, drinking too much in youth is a rite of passage, but it carries dangers and this story could have all ended rather differently. So, whilst I feel this story must be told, not least because if I hadn't seen it with my own eyes, I wouldn't have believed it, but because it should serve as a warning to the next generation.

It was around 1990 and I had yet to start my career in the Civil Service but was earning some cash by working in a national clothing store in Blackpool. The store had not long been open and several experienced full-time employees had been sent down from Scotland to oversee its opening and establishing itself.

It wasn't a job I took particularly seriously but it was a means of making some money for the weekend whilst I continued with my A Level studies.

Having said that there was a real buzz within the store's team, several of whom had temporarily located down to Blackpool. There were frequent nights out and a real bond formed with the younger team members.

Steve had left home in 1988 to join the Royal Air Force and, following his training, was based at RAF Wyton in Cambridgeshire, where most of the remaining Canberra aircraft were located, Steve being attached to 180 Squadron. Every now and then Steve would get the train home to visit his parents in Cleveleys for a week off or just a long weekend, which inevitably meant that we would team up for a night out. On the weekend in question, I had a big Friday night out planned with the team from the clothes Store and I was caught somewhat by surprise when the house phone rang around 5pm on the Friday and it was Steve. 'Alright me old Mucker…. guess where I am', 'hi Steve, how the hell are you doing…. don't tell me you're back home?' I said with a mixture of surprise and delight. 'I bleeding well am and you and I are out tonight my friend!', replied Steve clearly chomping at the bit.

You need to remember, this was in the days before mobile phones and in any case I recall Steve had made a last-minute decision to return home, once he'd established that he wasn't on guard duty that weekend, a task rotated around the Airmen no matter what trade.

'Ah, superb. Err…. only problem is I'm already on a night out with the people from work' I replied, 'Oh, not to worry then', said Steve rather crestfallen. I quicky recovered the situation, 'just come along pal, we're going out in Blackpool. They won't mind, they're a great bunch'. 'Are you sure' came the response from Steve'. 'Absolutely. We're meeting in Scrooges Wine Bar at 7pm, just get the tram up and meet us there'. 'Bloody wine bar…..I disappear to the RAF and now you're drinking in trendy wine bars….where the chuff did it all go wrong McEvoy'. Steve only referred to my surname in full when there was disapproval. 'It's not my choice matey' I replied, 'I think it was one of the girls in the team'. Steve's ears must have pricked up, 'Oh…. there are a few girls going out then?', 'yes, quite a few I think' I replied, 'bloody wise choice that wine bar then' came the reply, whilst chuckling. 'I'll see you at 7pm' I advised Steve and with that we said cheerio and ended the call.

Having gotten ready I walked the 3 miles to the outskirts of the Town Centre where Scrooges wine Bar was located, which has sadly now been demolished. It was a beautiful summers evening. No jacket required. I reached the venue and climbed the staircase to the bar, which was located on the first floor of the building. I quite liked Scrooges, it had its own charm and was an alternative place to start an evening out. The only problem was that it sold a dazzling range of potent and strange wines that were like rocket fuel. For the unsuspecting client used to 3% Lager Beer the wine was notorious for blowing folk sky high. The range was wide and unusual. There were Cherry and Gooseberry wines and even a Birch tree wine and they could all kill an evening if you guzzled too much too quickly.

On entering the bar I found most of the clothing Store crew. The whole bar was wooden planked – the walls the floor and even the tables and chairs colour matched. It certainly felt quite different to all the other Pubs and Bars in town.

I gave some of my work colleagues a high-five, said hello to others and then went to the bar to order a beer. Yep....I'm not a big wine fan I'm afraid....but I could see that the rest of my work colleagues were already well into their first bottles. I explained to my work colleagues that my pal was up from the RAF for the weekend and would they mind if he tagged along? Obviously, they were more than happy for him to join the night out.

Soon enough Steve entered the bar and was one of the last to join the ensembled group of about 12 people. It was great to see him, 'alright McAttack…how we doing?' asked Steve warmly, 'bloody great' came my reply. 'Nice one getting away from the base for the weekend' I added, 'I'll say…managed to wangle out of guard duty' said Steve with glee. After a handshake and pat on the back I introduced him to my work colleagues, which included Tom one of the Supervisors who was temporarily located down at the Blackpool Store from Glasgow.

Having made the introductions Steve and myself wandered over to the bar to get him a drink. 'You want one of these beers Steve' I asked, 'nah….we're in a wine bar…..what's the point in getting a beer? Here, look they sell Birch tree wine?! I'll have a bottle of that if you don't mind John' said Steve to the barman, whose real name was unknown and probably not John. I was a bit surprised, but who was I to argue. If Steve wanted wine, then fair enough. 'Do you want some McAttack….I'll get 2 glasses if you do', 'nah….not for me Steve, I hate the stuff. I'm a peasant I know but I'm going to stick with the beer. Thanks all the same'.

So, having purchased his Birch Tree wine we went and joined the rest of the gang. Everything was going extremely well. Steve fitted in just great, which wasn't a surprise as he's very much a social creature and very much the extrovert. Steve doesn't tag along. You can leave him to his own devices and we both very much enjoyed engaging with people we've never met before. And sure enough, in no time he was independently deep in conversation with several of my work colleagues, whilst I got on chatting with others.

The group were spread over 3 large tables and had gotten comfy - there was certainly no urge to move on to another pub or bar and the first hour or so disappeared in no time. With myself only drinking a rather weak beer I noticed that the empty wine bottles were mounting up and Steve was already into his 2nd bottle! The noise levels had ratcheted up too and quite a few were clearly starting to show that the wine was getting the better of them. In particular Steve and Supervisor Tom were getting rather louder than most…indeed Tom was swaying a little and it crossed my mind that some of the staff on detached duty in Blackpool and stopping in a nearby hotel had probably started a little earlier than the rest of us who had to get into the town centre area. It was around this point that I could see Steve and Tom were talking rather loudly.

I then heard Tom say, 'So you think you're the man eh', and Steve reply, 'there's not a Scotsman on the planet I couldn't drink under the table'. Eeek. This wasn't looking too rosy. 'Steve, just leave it, I think we've all had enough wine don't you think' I interjected. Tom turned to me, 'there's no stress Greg, no issue….we're just gonna find out who's the man'. By now the developing situation had grabbed everyone's attention and there were mutterings of 'don't be stupid guys' from some of the women. But nothing was going to stop the 2 Alpha males whose trajectory was on a collision course. There was a duel coming whether anyone else wanted it or not.

It was like the famous scene from Indiana Jones where there is a drink off. Steve one end of the table and Tom at the other. They took it in turns to gulp glasses of Birch tree, Cheery and Gooseberry wines.

The 2nd bottles were finished and 3rd bottles ordered. It was ridiculous. Those around the table watching with less sense and not wary to the consequences of excessive alcohol drinking were whooping and a hollering with every gulp. I do wonder to this day why the bar-staff never interjected? Maybe because the bar around us had filled up with it being a Friday evening and they were too busy to see what was going on? The drink-off continued unabated and the condition of both contestants deteriorated quickly....both gagged at times as if they might be sick.

Eventually Steve got to his last glass of his 3rd bottle and downed it in one, turning the empty wine glass upside down on the table to indicate he'd completed the mission. There were many whoops and shouts and pats on the back for Steve.

Steve looked green and Tom sozzled. And then I saw something I shall never forget and don't really want to see again. Tom pushed the last glass of wine in front of him into the middle of the table but then stood up. It was as if he were indicating to Steve that before he drank his last glass, he was capable of standing up.

The messaging was covert but obvious to me.... perhaps not to others i.e. I'm the last man standing. I was after all definitely the most sober there!

Silence fell amongst the group. Tom starred at Steve momentarily and Steve, along with everyone else, starred back at Tom. There was a sense something was going to happen. And then, without warning Tom collapsed face first slam into the table. He didn't flinch. No arms out, just headlong into the table, definitely a case of timbeerrrrrrrr. The table gave way, bottles and glasses flew everywhere; the group gasped in shock. Women screamed. The bar staff ran over. Thankful Tom hadn't hurt himself in the fall and wasn't out cold. But he was starting to wretch so was quickly taken under each arm by the bar staff to the toilet where he could get the 3 bottles of wine out of his system. Other bar-staff were quick to straighten tables and sweep up broken glass. They didn't moan, they just got on with it. Maybe they had seen what their wine could do before!

But I had no time to reflect on any of this. All of a sudden Steve got to his feet. He had remained seated whilst the commotion had gone on and the attentions had quite rightly been on Tom. Once on his feet Steve gave me a glance like a burglar might give a Policeman when caught red handed……..and then he shot off like the proverbial Hare. He just ran like a bullet to the exit. I have never seen Steve run so fast. 'Oh no' I exclaimed, putting my beer down and running as fast as I could after Steve. I knew he was completely bladdered…. definitely the worst I'd ever seen him and thus a danger to himself. I had no time for goodbyes and just ran.

On reaching the exit there was a very steep staircase and I just managed to glimpse Steve falling the last 5 or 6 steps and landing in a heap at the bottom. But he had a wine jacket on (instead of the usual beer jacket) and clearly had no concept of what he was doing nor any pain. He jumped to his feet and shot off out into the fresh air.

He ran off in the direction of Blackpool Tower but thankfully I had him in my sights, albeit 200 metres ahead of me. It was like a Police pursuit but Steve was shouting random things like 'Wahoo…..I'm the night fairy'. God only knows what people walking by must have thought?

And so, we ran on past the Winter Gardens, down past the Hounds Hill Shopping Centre and then past the entrance to the Blackpool Tower, all the time myself shouting 'Steve, Steve hold-up'. But it was no use, he was clearly in another world and the fresh air on top of the ridiculous amount of wine had a devastating and dangerous effect.

Then my worst fears materialised as Steve shot-up the wide and extensive staircase that led to the famous Palace Nightclub. However, the same staircase also led to a bridge that took pedestrians over the road outside the Tower onto the promenade. At the time the road immediately outside the Tower was a dual carriageway. This was changed in later years down to a single lane in both directions but at the time the bridge was much-needed to get the tourist hoard's safely across an exceptionally busy road.

Having sprinted up the staircase as fast as I could, I found Steve on the bridge but now on the wrong side of the railings. He'd climbed over and was now holding onto the rails with only his toes on the main structure of the bridge. He was swinging and shouting, 'Wahoo…..look at me…. I'm a fairy and I can fly'. I was scared and shouted at Steve as I neared, 'NO! You're NOT a fairy and you can't fly…..give me your hand now' I demanded. I knew before long someone would call the Police fearing someone was looking to jump! Steve continued, 'I can fly look I can fly' as he dangerously swung on the railing on the wrong side perilously close to ending his life.

It wasn't a time for messing about and I was angry with myself for allowing Steve to get into a stupid drink-off with Tom. We'd been in enough scrapes in our time but we were best mate and I wasn't going to let it all end here. I grabbed both of Steve's arms and pulled hard so that he came in closer to the railings and shouted at him like I'd never spoken to him before or since, 'get your backside over here NOW you blithering idiot'. I had a rage in my face and despite being a little drunk my demeanour must have pierced through somehow. Steve looked me in the eye, 'enough fun for one day then'? he said pathetically and slurring his words, 'you're bloody right it's been enough for a month. Get on the other side of the railings NOW'. Still holding onto Steve tightly he gingerly climbed over the railings onto the path that led across the bridge.

He was safe and I breathed a sigh of relief. 'I fink I'm a bit squiffy' said Steve who was swaying all over the place, 'squiffy.....squiffy....you're bloody more that squiffy you moron! You've had 3 bottles of wine you pillock. I'm getting you home'.

I escorted Steve to the promenade end of the bridge and down the stairs, which seemed to take forever as he navigated one step at a time. There are always plenty of taxis on Blackpool Promenade and I was able to quickly hail one over. I negotiated a price for Steve and paid the taxi driver but not before explaining that he was exceptionally drunk and giving the driver Steve's mum and dads address. I gave the driver some extra money perchance Steve vomited in the taxi on the way home. As it transpires this didn't happen.....never did get that fiver back!

I walked home, the night having been curtailed a little. I had no appetite to go back and find out what was happening with Tom, the others could deal with him. In fact, I don't recall seeing Tom ever again after that night. Maybe he returned to Scotland?

On reaching home both my parents were still up, 'hi son, you're a lot earlier than usual, good night', 'yeah, just a couple of quiet ones with Steve. He'd been travelling most of the day up from Cambridgeshire so was tired. You know he needs his sleep'. If only they knew! And with that I took myself off to bed for an early night.

The next day came and I was a bit worried about how Steve might be but I decided to leave things until later in the day. I called Steve's house around 4pm in the afternoon and his mum, Val, answered. 'Oh, hi Greg, are you ok', 'yes, I'm fine thanks Val' I replied. 'Well Steve's in a terrible way. What on earth did he drink last night? He's had his head down the toilet most of the night and morning! I've NEVER known him like this? I hope he's not taken anything else'. She was clearly worried. 'No, it's just booze Val. We went to a wine Bar and he ended up in a drinking competition with someone he didn't know. Not sure he's used to the wine to be honest'. 'The bloody idiot' replied Val, 'well, serves him right then, that's the day written off for him! He must have drunk a ridiculous amount as Bill and myself have never seen him like that before. It can be really dangerous getting that drunk you know'. And she was right. If only she knew……..and let this be a warning to the next generation!

CHAPTER 5 – THE BITS WAINWRIGHT MISSED DAY I
Seal – Crazy

I learnt to drive as soon as I reached the age of 17 and that was a bit of a game changer because the world literally became our Oyster. I'd also learnt to fly motorised gliders with the Air Training Corps at age 16, which seemed mighty young and being able to fly before you could legally drive felt odd. But I wasn't complaining!

My first car was a rather boring blue Vauxhall Chevette, but it was nippy, in good condition and reliable. Not long after learning to drive the dynamic duo hatched a plan to get away for a weekend in the English Lake District, which was only an hour away from Blackpool. We were lucky to be so close to such a stunning part of the country. The days seemed to drag by in getting to our much-awaited weekend, but eventually it arrived and we couldn't wait to get going. A weekend of joy and utter mayhem lay ahead that lives long in the memory. There is no doubt in my mind that this particularly weekend helped forge our friendship and was a great adventure.

The car was loaded with our overnight bags, Steve's mum having passed me his holdall on arrival at his house so I could place it in the car boot. It was like she wanted him out from under her feet! I sat in Steve's front living room waiting whilst he dried his hair and got changed. I was itching to get going and really excited but as per usual Steve was taking his time. I was pretty sure our adventures were going to new levels this coming weekend.....I waited impatiently. Steve's mum,

Val, made some small talk to pass the time, 'so do you know where you're going when you get there Greg', she asked? 'Errm no' I replied, the usual amount of planning had gone into the project, 'we're definitely going to Bowness on Windermere but no, we've nothing booked. I'm sure we'll be fine'. Val sat in the armchair opposite with Tina, the pet dog, getting all her attention, 'well…. it's not too far, only an hour away. I guess if you don't find anywhere you can always come home'. Ha! *Fat chance of that* I thought to myself. No way Jose! We were going to be on it like a car bonnet, as Steve would say.

After waiting what felt like an interminable amount of time Steve appeared. God only knows why it takes him so long to get ready. 'Right bugger-lugs' he said with aplomb and hands dramatically clasped together, 'are we ready to hit the road chump'? I stood up, 'damn right I am. Let's get going' I replied, already walking towards the living room door. Steve gave his mum a kiss on the cheek to say goodbye, with 'be careful… both of you' her parting instruction that we ignored as we headed out the front door to my blue chariot that was sat primed, ready for launch. We jumped in the car and Steve's mum walked out to the brick wall that marked the end of the garden, in order to wave us off. 'Quick' said Steve. 'wind the window down'. I put the window down as requested by which point Steve had slammed a Bonjovi Tape into the cassette player and tuned the volume to max, 'YOU'RE LOVE IS LIKE BAD MEDICINE…..' came blasting out so loud that it scared the pants off me! I wrestled to turn it down as the local idiot pulled my hand away, 'leave it, leave it' he said laughing away to himself, '…and step on it' he shouted above the racket. Val looked on shaking her head, 'you're a bloody pair of plonkers you two' she shouted towards the open window as we sped off. She wasn't wrong! I'm sure I could see faces appearing at the neighbour's netted curtains, peaking to find out what all the commotion was about?! I'm not sure whether the expressions etched on their faces were of concern for the din, or of joy that we were clearing off! Good Job Steve's Dad Bill was at work, otherwise he'd have had something to say for sure. Probably pillocks!

I hit the accelerator to the floor and we shot off down Westmorland Road like we'd just done a bank job. Once round the corner and out of sight I slowed down, wound the window up and turned the music down. 'Right McAttack, let's hit that road and go and have us a party', said Steve riddled with excitement, 'damn right' came my reply and we headed for the M55 exit near Kirkham. The journey to the Lake District and, in our case Windermere and Bowness, is extremely straight forward - M55, M6 and then the A590/591 all the way. It was a Friday morning and also after rush hour, so the roads were light on traffic. It was also a beautiful summers day. We donned our sun glasses and sat back to enjoy the drive north. 'Steve, take that BonJovi cassette out. I've been saving up my Disco crisp tokens and managed to get a new album for free', I said with much pride. I'd eaten a ridiculous number of Disco crisps and scrounged empty packets that weren't mine whilst at college (I'm a peasant I know) in order attain the prerequisite number of tokens needed to get a free Album. I'd plumbed for Seal who had just released a new album of the same name, with hits such as *Crazy*. 'Oh, cool' said Steve taking the cassette from me and putting it into the player. I think it's fair to say *that was that*. The Album defined the whole weekend and we played it every time we got in the car. It is a truly amazing and unique Album. Whenever either of us hear a track from that Album, it takes me back to that weekend, to a time and a place. A most wonderful time in our lives. I'm sure people reading this perhaps have a certain song or maybe an album that is the same for them. That brings a memory flooding back. Good or bad.

Unlike some folk heading in the same direction towards the Lake District, our car was not loaded with tents, sleeping bags, hiking boots, Kayaks, stoves and other such outward-bound paraphernalia. Nope. All we had was an overnight bag each with a couple of shirts, swimming shorts and fresh underwear. Food, beer and fun on the water was all we had in mind. Steve has never been one for too much exertion, and climbing mountain peaks was definitely not on his bucket list! I was happy to go with the flow, very much a case of rolling the dice and seeing what would happen. I should add that in the early 1990's the speed restrictions that they now have on Lake Windermere hadn't been applied and thus water-skiing and misbehaving in speed boats was still very much allowed.

Before we knew it, we were off the M6 and passing Kendal and, not much longer after that coming into Windermere itself. The excitement was building and we were both intrigued as to where we might find ourselves staying for the evening. It was the summer so pretty busy and there was no guarantee that we would find somewhere to stop. Having driven through Windermere itself we carried on driving, eventually dropping down a pretty steep hill into Bowness until we eventually came to the Lake shore. It was rammed jammed with tourists eating ice-creams and queuing to catch a boat ride in one of the flotilla of small boats that charge a small fortune to sail up and down the longest Lake in England....all 12 miles of it, whilst taking in breath-taking scenery. The largest of these boats is The Swan, which to this day still plies its trade up and down the water. Thankfully we were extremely lucky to find an empty parking space adjacent to the jetties where the boats departed and very close by the Tourist Information office.

Having parked and locked the car we headed off at a pace towards the Tourist Information office, whilst gawping at the splendid looking Belsfield Hotel painted in white high up on a hill immediately above us. It looked wonderful but was definitely out of our price range. On reaching the Tourist Information Office and queuing for a short while to be served, our enquiries for suggestions on suitable accommodation got us nowhere, 'you'll just have to speculate lads. There are loads of B&B's, just go looking.

This is the best place to start. Where are you from'? 'Blackpool' replied Steve, 'agh, well, if you don't find anywhere it's only an hour down the road to get home'.

That was the 2nd time in one morning I'd heard that! Steve and I looked at one another but said nothing as the telepathy kicked in. *Fat chance*!

And so, we left the Tourist Information Office less than impressed but undeterred into the warm sunshine looking for somewhere to stop for the next 2 nights. The vast majority of places were displaying signs saying *'No Vacancies'*. Those that did not were a little too expensive if not *Boutique* for the likes of Steve and myself and at least one proprietor advised he didn't take all male parties. Oh well. We were looking for something cheap and cheerful, but this was proving much harder than we had expected. Eventually Steve found a rather grand looking Victorian Terrace B&B that said Vacancies in the window. We walked up the steps and rang the bell BING…..BONG….. came the sound in a delayed fashion. A gentleman opened the door with a handlebar moustache, 'yes lads' he enquired. Steve, did the talking. 'Errm…..hi. I wonder if you can help us. We're looking for a room for the night'. The man didn't respond but rather turned and shouted though to someone else in the house, '…..have we still got those rooms or have they gone'?

A voice shouted back, 'they never turned up and haven't bothered to call….so as far as I'm concerned sod them. So yes, they're available'. The man turned back to us, 'well, well boys. It looks like you're in luck after all. A party hasn't turned so we're a couple of rooms free'. Steve and myself looked at each other, 'agh great' we said in unison. The man looked us up and down, 'what you be wanting then, a double or singles'? The pair of us froze. Like we'd seen a ghost. Weighing up whether we'd heard right or not! Had someone just asked if we wanted to share a bed? I should add that neither Steve or myself are homophobic but we were best pals and aghast that we'd been asked. You could have knocked us down with a feather duster! 'Single, single, yes single, most definitely single' we said scrambling in unison and rather cutting across one another. 'We've been best mates since kids' I qualified…….just to be on the safe side. 'How much is the room' asked Steve, '£37 boys per night' came the reply. 'Ahh, a little more than we planned' said Steve quickly. 'Thanks anyway for your time' and with that we were off down the steps and scurried round the corner and into the main street laughing to ourselves, 'a double!' I exclaimed, 'Hells bells' said Steve, 'who'd want to share a bed with you!' We stopped bent double laughing, tears rolling down our faces. 'Come on McAttack……there are more B&B's further away from the lake shore up the main hill. I spotted them on the drive down.

Let's go and have a look'. And with that we strode off up

cardiac hill knocking on various B&B doors, two of which were Pub's, but only to be disappointed time and time again. We were both starting to seriously think that we were going to be out of luck and have to head off home.

However, at the top of the hill and down a side street, we found a small B&B called *Robin's Nest*. We rang the doorbell and a man in his mid-thirties wearing a blue sweater opened the door, 'we're looking for a room for a couple of nights, don't suppose you have anything available'. 'Yeah, sure, I've got a twin room if you want it, come in lads and see what you think' said the man in a warm and friendly manner'. 'Thought we were going to be out of luck' I said to the man, 'everywhere is booked up'. The man smiled, 'well as it happens, we aren't actually open for business. My wife is expecting any day so we decided to close but seeing as you're here you're more than welcome and besides, we could do with the cash with a little one on the way'. Steve interjected, 'we wouldn't want to impose if your wife is expecting......' , but before he could finish his sentence the man put his hand up as if to gesture Steve to stop. 'No, no. It's fine lads. Here's the room' and with that he showed us into what had previously been a front room just off the hallway that had been turned into a bedroom. It was clean, very large and had 2 single beds. It was also right next to the front door, so getting home late wouldn't disturb anyone else and it wasn't far from the pubs and restaurants. Even better it was only £20 per night. Steve and myself looked at each other and nodded. It was perfect. 'Great. We'll take it' said Steve. The man then took us through to the communal kitchen where his wife was sat precariously holding onto her huge belly. She was clearly at full term and ready to give birth any day. As we entered the kitchen, she said hello and then stood up to waddle around looking for something.

A huge farm house stye dining table dominated the centre of the room on a very old looking stone floor. The man followed us into the kitchen, 'make yourself at home boys. The fridge is full of food for a fry-up and cereal is over here. Here's a key for you. All I ask is that you try and keep the noise down if coming in late. Also, if perchance we're not here come Sunday morning i.e. I've had to rush my wife into Kendal hospital to give birth, then just post the key back through the letter box'. Steve interjected with genuine concern, 'are you really sure you're ok about us stopping here? It looks like you've enough on'. 'Absolutely', came the reply. 'Where are you from lads' he asked, 'Blackpool' we said together. 'Agh well. Not too far away then. What could go wrong with 2 lads from Blackpool'. We shot a glance sideways at one another......he clearly hadn't met the likely lads before. And with that we graciously took the key and headed to our room to check it out further, wishing his expectant wife all the very best.

We quickly decided who was having which bed and then set off back down the hill to fetch the car back to the B&B and unpack. Enroute we took in our surroundings a little more, clocking the various restaurants, takeaways, pubs and shops. As we walked along in the glorious sunshine we chatted, so what's the plan over the next 2 days Steve?' I asked. 'Well, we're booked in to water-ski centre at 2pm so we need to drive down the water sports place in another hour really. Then we can come back and get something to eat, sink a few beers and hit the Clubs'. 'Clubs....I don't think there are any nightclubs here', 'yeah there is, there's one....and it's right there', said Steve with confidence and pointing to a large grey building on the shore next to the pier jetties. And sure enough he was right. There it was, the Starlite Nightclub, open until 2am the sign proudly declared. Magic. That was us sorted for the evening then. Steve continued, 'so how about tomorrow, after we shake-off the inevitable hangover, we buy some throw away BBQ's, get some food and go and find a spot where we can cook some food down on the shore, maybe swim in the lake'. I liked the sound of that. 'Great idea Steve' I said smiling all the while. And off we marched to find my car. However, the inevitable 'are you hungry' question came from Steve before we reached said vehicle. Steve had clearly caught a whiff of the Fish and Chip restaurant a few doors down from the nightclub. Hence, we filled our faces with pudding, sausage, chips and gravy so our bellies were fully loaded for the afternoon's exertion that lay ahead of us.

Having recovered my car, we drove back to the B&B where we parked up and unpacked our bags. Steve pulled 2 bottles of beer from his bag, which were cracked open in no time and he passed me one, 'here's to the weekend'. 'I'll drink to that. Let's have a belter'. And down the hatch they went. But only the 1 for next we were off to the water sports centre.

It was only a short drive to the water sports centre, so we got there in no time. Times have changed since the lake speed restrictions were introduced in 2005. Up until that point the Lake was awash with speedboats and jet skis of every description. It was a throng of high-speed activity for the thrill seeker.

The aim of the speed restrictions was to restore the lake's tranquillity but at the time it faced severe criticism from some lake users. You can make your own mind up.

Back in 1991, during the time of our visit, there was a real market in this niche water sports sector and some serious money was being made. As we pulled into the car park, we hid our blue Vauxhall chariot right at the back, away from the Porches, Ferraris, Bentleys and such like vehicles. I kid you not. On walking round the main building and getting shore side the serious money continued on the water with a dazzling number of extremely powerful Mastercraft Speedboats to be had. It certainly felt like a playground for the wealthy. There must have been some puzzled looks as the likely lads turned up in their Bermuda shorts!

Having settled up for the cost of the water-skiing session and donned our rental wet suits and life jackets we trotted off after our driver and instructor for the afternoon. We walked down a long and narrow wooden jetty that was lined with some truly amazing looking boats. Ours was moored at the end of the jetty and was a very large and stunningly shiny red Mastercraft Speedboat. It was trimmed with chrome and had white leather-look interior. Very nice indeed. We were impressed. The 3 of us donned our shades and jumped aboard. In no time our driver untied the moorings, started the engine and, once a few yards off the jetty, we tore off like a house on fire, with the two of us getting flung back into our seats. A bit of showing off I'm sure from the driver!

The driver had explained before setting off that we would make our way to a quieter part of the lake before we started, with me being a novice. Steve had explained that he was pretty experienced. I was intrigued to see how this played out.

I have a vivid memory of Steve and myself sat in that boat, tearing down Lake Windermere, on a stunningly hot summer afternoon, the wind blasting our hair backwards. Not a word was exchanged for the din of the boat's engines.....but not a care in the world we had. I think, for a brief moment, we even thought we were Bay Watch! The Lake was alive, a throng of activity and we waved to people on yachts, in their sailing dinghys, canoes, wind surfers and the passing tourist boats. The world was ours and I don't think we would have wanted to be anywhere else. A treasured moment of youth.

After a pretty decent run down the lake, our instructor hit a hard left and we headed towards a designated area for water skiing. We held on for dear life as we were literally thrown from one side of the speedboat to the other. The instructor looked over; it was all smiles. All of a sudden, the boat throttled right back, the wind in our hair dwindled and we came to an abrupt halt, with the engines at idle. 'Right, you want to go first and show him how it's done…..give me a thumbs up when you're ready', said the instructor to Steve. 'Yep, let's do it' came Steve's reply and within a flash he'd jumped into the lake, his sleek buoyancy aid bringing him to the surface rather quickly. The instructor threw Steve 2 large water skis, much larger than what you might use for snow skiing. They had a rubber fitting to slide your feet in. Steve donned them with little fuss and gave a thumbs up with his right hand whilst holding on to the large handle tied to the tow rope with his left. I was impressed……maybe he wasn't blagging after all! The engines roared and off we went like a bullet. Being the complete amateur once again I was flung flying into the bottom of the boat, much to the amusement of the instructor.

Once I'd righted myself, I glanced towards Steve. I was in awe. There he was some 25 yards away going hell for leather, zipping sideways with elegance, hitting the wake behind the speedboat and jumping through the air landing with some style as he continued his run on the other side of the boat.

Steve took one of his hands off the bar and gave me the thumbs up and a short wave. I waved back and smiled. This was superb. I was quite happy to sit there and watch Steve, whist taking in the breath-taking scenery.

On a day like this, with such stunning weather, we truly could have been on Lake Maggiore in Italy. After a good 20minutes of blasting up and down the designated section of the lake and with only one fall by Steve, the boat again slowed down, turned and then drew up alongside Steve. There was a plinth at water level at the back of this boat, especially designed to make it easier for the water skier to climb aboard. Steve crawled aboard, dripping from head to toe, 'wow….you were pretty awesome out there pal….I gotta hand it to you, 'agh, no sweat, like I say, I've been several times before with my uncle. Now let's see what you can do McAttack'! The instructor, come driver, had stood up and moved away from his driving seat. He started to lift a large grey steel bar and attach it to the side of the boat.

It protruded out sideways and looked like something a trapeze artist might use! 'What the hell is that' I said out loud, not aiming my question at anyone in particular. 'It's to help you get used to skiing with an aid before we let you loose on the rope, with you being a learner', said the instructor sympathetically. 'Let me qualify that for you. Basically, it's a retards bar' said Steve, bringing it right back down. 'Agh, great, I'm gonna look like a right plonker on the end of that aren't I', 'no, not at all' said the instructor again sympathetically. 'No…..you're going to look like a right muppet….and I can't wait to see you go for a burton…..right shall we get on with it John' said Steve, already chomping at the bit to see my attempt and chuckling away to himself.

I gingerly lowered myself into the water to Steve's shouts of *get in there you tart*, or words to that effect. Despite the wetsuit it still felt cold. I was thrown the water skis, which I struggled for a good 5-minutes trying to fit. With the buoyancy aid lifting my torso up and the need to also raise my legs made it quite a challenge. But eventually I had my skis on and the speedboat opened up its engines to tear round in a loop to bring the beginners bar alongside, which I managed to grab firmly with both arms. 'OK, ARE YOU READY' shouted the driver over the din of the engines, 'JUST ABOUT THANKS', 'OK.....listen up, as we set off try and straighten your back and pull yourself upwards keeping those legs together. You got that'? 'Yes...lets rock and roll' I replied. Hmm. What followed wasn't exactly *rock and roll* that's for sure. The speedboat shot off, I got 3 feet up and then SLAM face down into the ice-cold water. I looked up and Steve was bent double laughing. Even the driver was laughing. Second attempt....SLAM face down.......third attempt......SLAM face down.....4th attempt....and he's up and away!! There I was holding on to the beginners bar....bent double like a granny holding onto her supermarket trolley for dear life in a gale. It wasn't pretty and Steve and the instructor both took great amusement from my precarious ski posture, but I didn't care. I was up and doing it and that was all that mattered. After a few falls and a gradual improvement in my posture, the boat came to a halt, 'time for the real thing then' shouted our instructor and I was thrown the rope. I grabbed the handle at the end firmly. And off we went full pelt.....hey presto...I was up! I rather fancied I was up for crossing over the wake to the other side of the lake like Steve, so not to be outdone I leant inwards. The speed increased dramatically and I looked just the pro as we passed a boat with some rather nice young ladies aboard smiling over. Whoops. Loss in concentration. SLAM and an explosion of water followed by disorientation.

Where was I, where's the boat? Then sure enough the speedboat pulled up alongside me, Steve holding onto his belly with laugher and even the instructor who'd probably seen such a fall many times before.

The eejit in the back was laughing his proverbial socks off, 'what you doing trying to do that first time round, you absolute pillock! Right in front of those girls! Trying to show off were we', said Steve now smirking. He had me. But what fun. What an afternoon. After another 10 minutes of water skiing and our time was up. I joined my partner in crime in the back of the boat for some manic, exhilarating driving from the instructor on our way back to the ski school base. A truly memorable afternoon. Having showered and dressed we thanked our instructor and headed for the car, 'come on McAttack, let's head back to Bowness….you hungry'?

Once back in Bowness it was late afternoon and the throng had reduced considerably as the day trippers left, leaving only locals and those staying in the town. Remarkably, we were even able to park right outside the B&B that we had found only a few hours earlier. 'Right…..let's get straight on it….bite to eat and some beers methinks' said Steve with great aplomb.
I couldn't disagree, so we quickly got changed into attire that would see us out for the whole evening and set off down into Bowness to find a good Pub. We soon found the Village Inn, a fantastic Pub located at the heart of Bowness and not far from the Lake shore. The Pub became synonymous with Moosehead lager beer for us as it was on offer at the time. A great beer made by the Canadian brewing giant Labatt's. I'm

not sure either of us had drunk Moosehead before, but let's just say that we consumed a significant amount and in the years to come each time we passed the Village Inn, we'd say 'Moosehead' in unison! Indeed, it's one of the first things we recall about the weekend. I can't really remember what we ate but eat we did. After a while we spotted a bench that had become free, where we went and sat in the sun watching the world go, quietly burning ourselves in the sun. Absolutely perfect.

After we'd been there way too long, we headed off on a mini-pub crawl. We were by now *well on our way* and I sure as hell couldn't tell you where we went or who we spoke to....and besides, it is such a long-time ago now. But invariably we did end up talking to folk and it was usually outside given it was such a glorious evening.

The day having turned to night and Pub closing time nearing, Steve suggested that we head towards The Starlite Nightclub, 'come on McAttack, let's get to that Club and meet some ladies' he said with a belch. Nice. Looking at the pair of us I didn't fancy our chances. We were both bladdered, sun burnt and the water skiing, whilst fun, had been exhausting. It wasn't lost on me though that Steve was truly inebriated and hell bent on going. So off we went down to the water edge where the nightclub was located. Once paid up and allowed in, it was clear that all the lasses that had come to the Lake District for a healthy weekend fell walking or doing water sports were of a mind to have an early night. The venue seemed to be predominantly full of blokes who'd had too much in the boozers and looking for a few more. Don't forget, this was in a time when Pubs closed at 23:00 and the nightclub at 02:00! However, the night was not done. 'Having just bought us a pint of lager each - like we needed more ale - Steve flung his glass in front of me, 'here...hold this whilst I dance'. What the....?! And, whilst I stood rather drunk at the side nursing two cold pints of lager amongst the physic teachers and rugby player types, Steve strutted onto the dance floor, which up until that point only had 3 middle age women dancing around their handbags to Chaka Khan. Unbeknown to me Steve had slipped off to make a request to the DJ enroute to the bar.

Now, when you're really, really drunk in a nightclub, I can tell you that there is nothing quite as surreal and that brings you quickly to your senses as watching your best mate commandeer 24square foot of a dance floor and windmill dance to Tiffany, *I think we're alone now*. My jaw hit the floor and the old sorts already on the dance floor looked over their shoulder pads with partial concern and disgust as they shuffled nearer the edge of the dance floor away from the nutter now breaking his moves, for fear of being *taken out*! The last time I saw someone dancing like that was on an old video footage of the Woodstock festival in America!

I wasn't sure if Steve was having some kind of fit or outer body experience.....or both! One thing is for sure....he looked like a right twit. After allowing John Travolta a little more time to entertain himself and with the song drawing to a close, I did what all good mates do. I put the pints down and grabbed him, 'long day tomorrow Steve, there are no lasses in here and you're gonna kill someone with that dancing. Time to go methinks'. Steve was totally hammered, but saw the light, 'yep. Let's go', and with that he skulled his pint in one and off he strode at a pace towards the exit.

GREG MCEVOY

Tomorrow was indeed going to be a long and glorious day and we'd certainly consumed more than enough for one evening. But what a magical day we'd had.

CHAPTER 6 – THE BITS WAINWRIGHT MISSED DAY II
Seal – Future Love Paradise

The next morning the dynamic duo woke with the inevitable fuzz……the predicable hangover. I lay momentarily thinking 'where am I', before realising I was in the Lake District on a weekend with my pal Steve. I sat up and looked over towards Steve who was stirring, 'oh man alive…….my head hurts' came the response from the single bed on the other side of the room, presumably having noted that I'd woken. 'You go and get showered McAttack and I'll go next and then let's get some breakfast', 'yeah Ok', I said coming to my senses and sliding out of bed to make my way to the communal bathroom. Given we were the only residents we had the place to ourselves, so we were able to trot along to the bathroom in our boxer shorts unhindered. 'Don't be lying in Steve', I said, as he was and still is renowned for taking ages to get ready, 'its glorious out there. Let's not waste the day in here', 'yeah, I'm with you… absolutely. I'll be right behind you', and with that I left Steve for a few more minutes snoozing, whilst I went to get washed and dressed. Remarkably Steve was true to his word and he found me in the kitchen for breakfast only 20 minutes after myself.

'What a cracking day yesterday was eh', 'yeah, it was brilliant, really enjoyed it matey'. Steve had come too and was energised and planning the day ahead, 'once we've had breakfast, I'll walk down to that Spar Shop at the bottom of the hill and buy us a load of food and some disposable BBQ's. It's hard to park down there, so if you give me say 20 mins to walk down, buy the gear and then I'll be waiting outside for you to pick me up in the car. Then we can just hit the road and go and find a spot to spend the day by the Lake. The walk down gives me time to clear my head too. How does that sound'? 'Yep, sounds like a plan to me. Make sure you're there though'. Remember, no mobile phones back in the early 90's, so you always had to be precise on the arrangements! 'Where are we going to go then Steve, any ideas?' I asked. 'No…..not really….but there are loads of places we could stop along Windermere, and there are other Lakes. We'll find somewhere'. As per usual we were just going to *roll the dice* and see what happened. As I've gotten older, I like a bit more certainty in what I'm going to be doing. However, the magic of youth is that the world is very much your oyster and you should just go with it and see where life takes you, that's what makes it magical.

After we had eaten, we went back to our room to pack a bag with swimming shorts, towels and some soft drinks we had purchased. We bumped into the landlord just as we were about to leave. 'Hi guys, good day yesterday'? 'Yes, brilliant thanks' we replied in unison. 'You get into the fells? asked the owner? 'No, out on the Lake, we went water skiing, then hit the town. Didn't get in until late as we ended up in the Club down by the Lake'. 'Oh, right. You certainly had a full day then! We didn't hear you coming in, so it must have been late'. 'How is your wife' I asked? 'She's still here. No change. Just a waiting game now'. Thanks for asking. Where you going today?' asked the landlord. 'Not sure, going to find a spot along the shore of Windermere or perhaps another Lake, have a BBQ, with the weather being so nice'. 'Well, I suggest you get yourselves over to Ullswater, take the back road via Troutbeck. Some great places down on the shoreline there.

It's a bit quieter than Windermere.....but after the night you two have just had you might appreciate it!', he said with a wry smile and a cheeky wink. Steve and myself looked at each other and nodded. Bingo. Now we had a plan. 'Agh, yes...... that sounds like what we're after. That's great, thanks for that. We'll give that a go. Cheers', replied Steve. And with that we left the B&B.

I loaded the boot and sat in the car for 20 minutes listening to Seal - what an album that is - whilst Steve made his way down the hill to the Spar shop. For the first time I took in my surroundings. The B&B was one of several terrace houses. All made from locate slate stone and immaculate. The road was a cul-de-sac with a narrow turning space at the end, where there appeared to be some kind of workshop garage. Maybe a joiner? The row of Terrace housing sat in the shadow, the easterly morning sun yet to find its way round to this particular street. It did cross my mind that, given the properties were Easterly facing but on the downward slope of a westerly running hill, they might not get too much morning sunshine...ever. Maybe I was wrong?

I gave Steve longer than we'd planned. Having known him for a good few years by this point I knew that he operated to his own clock and any number of distractions might have waylaid him enroute. Eventually, after nearly 30minutes, I started up the Chevette, turned it around at the end of the cul-de-sac and made my way to the main road. It was only a very short drive, but a 10–15-minute walk by foot, hence allowing Steve the head start. I drove down the hill in no particular hurry. It was sometime after 9:30am on a truly stunning summers morning.

Once again Bowness had a continental feel about it. It could quite easily have been Switzerland or Italy. It was glorious. It wasn't particularly busy, with a small number of people walking about on morning strolls, getting the morning paper, or sat outside cafeterias having a cappuccino.

I came down the steep hill slowly given there was no traffic behind me and there he was, stood on the opposite side of the road, as planned. So far so good. However, my jaw dropped when I looked at how much shopping he had bought... 'Oh... My....God' ran through my mind, I swear it looked as if he'd done the weekly shop. Steve stood there and waved me over like a taxi and, lying around his feet on the ground, there must have been approximately 12 white Spar carrier bags. As arranged with Steve, I turned around at the bottom of the hill and came back up the left-hand side of the road to collect Steve. I pulled up alongside him and put the handbrake on as hard as I could, now pinned back in my seat like an airline passenger on take-off given the steepness of the hill. There was a grin like a Cheshire cat across his face as he swiftly pulled the door open. 'Right McAttack.....I've got us SOOO much stuff, we'll be sorted for the day. Just let me pop it in the boot'. I shook my head in disbelief, 'yeah...Redman strikes again....eyes bigger than his belly... looks like you've just bought the bloody shop! How much have you spent in there....and who else is coming....that looks ridiculous?!'. Steve laughed, 'ha ha. You know me. Better to have too much than too little and don't worry about the money. We'll sort that another time' he said with relish. Once the boot was loaded and slammed shut Steve jumped in the car. 'Stunning morning isn't it. Right. Let's go and find us that Lake Mr McEvoy' he said and, with the engine still running I removed the handbrake and gave it plenty of gas so as to get away up the very steep hill climb out of Bowness.

Once on the road and out of the Town I had to ask Steve what on earth he had bought? 'So, what have you gotten us'? 'Well, to be honest I've probably gone a bit overboard, but what we don't need we can take home. I got us burgers, sausages, Chinese Pork Steaks, Steak, salad, rolls, pop…..thought we'd stay off the beer until later….crisps, potato salad, sausage rolls, mini-party sausages, savoury salad, pasta, couscous, chocolate cake, cheese cake, mousse, Mars Bars and 3 disposable BBQ's…oh….and some matches to light them and some BBQ utensils and some disposable plates. Oh, and the Daily Sport'. I looked at him incredulously, 'Couscous! Are you out of your tiny mind'?!, as if the Couscous was the tipping point and taken things too far. 'Well, we are going to be there for the full day aren't we…..so some couscous might be needed'. There was a momentary silence and then we both bust out laughing.

Once out of Bowness and then Windermere Steve, using the obligatory Roadmap that everyone had in those days (no Sat Nav back then), directed me towards the road that would take us to Ullswater. It looked a minor A road and not a major throughfare, 'are you sure this is the way Steve, looks like a back country lane to me', 'yep…..I'm sure McAttack. Trust me, I'm your best mate. This is the way, step on it and turn the music up', and there we were blasting along a tight and winding road on an amazing summers morning towards Ullswater with Seal singing his hit *Crazy* as we went. And Crazy indeed it was. A few short miles into the countryside, with us belting along at a fare pace and singing along to Crazy, I took a left-hand bend perhaps a little faster than I should have done. At the time of writing these memoirs I've now known Steve for over +35 years. But it nearly ended on that day...and on that bend. In all the years since we've been in a few scrapes, but the dynamic duo were lucky on this day. As I hit the bend at around 50mph, on a road I'd never driven on before, I found it was much tighter than I'd anticipated and I was on the white line braking hard.

As we hit the apex of the bend a white Volkswagen Beetle was exactly on the same trajectory. I couldn't say for sure, but I think it was also a young man and, like myself had probably not appreciated how tight the bend was. In a split second I pulled hard left with everything I had and so did the Beetle driver. By the grace of god, we missed by millimetres. Had it not been a red-hot morning and the road offering a good grip then it would have been curtains for Steve and I, of that I have no doubt. Had it been wet, as it is for the vast majority of the year in the English Lake District, then I doubt I'd be writing this now. Once out of the bend I slammed hard on the brakes and pulled over.

Our hearts were pounding. I was in shock but I also wanted to see if the guy in the other car was ok? We both got out of the car and looked at the bend from where we had just come. But now, in the distance, we could see the White Beetle merrily driving along. We had expected that he might also have stopped. 'Maybe he didn't appreciate just how close that was' I said, now feeling a little relieved that the occupants of both vehicles were ok and that the white Beetle hadn't ended up in a field or down a ravine on the other side. 'Who knows', replied Steve thoughtfully, 'you ok pal' he asked. 'Yeah, I'm OK. But that was really, really close. I'm sorry pal'. And I was. I've never had such a close call since that incident. May it serve as a warning to my own children and Steve's.

Always take care on roads that you are unfamiliar with. Steve laughed….but only half joking… 'look, if you're going to kill me, let me at least let me get to my 21st!!'. And with that we jumped into the car and continued down the A592 towards the village of Glenridding on Ullswater…..at a considerably slower speed! The car's brakes were tested even further as we descended the long, winding and exceptionally steep road down towards Ullswater through Kirkstone pass.

Eventually we reached Glenridding, which was beautiful, with a wonderful Victorian Hotel on the Lake shore. However, it was rammed with people. We could clearly see a water sports centre of the non-powered variety, with kayaks, canoes, small dinghys etc, and it seemed like a significant amount of people were going to take advantage of these pleasure crafts for hire on this amazingly hot day. Many had brought their own and this seemed to be a recognised launch spot. But that wasn't what Steve and myself were looking for. Living in Blackpool we were used to the hordes of tourists, so we were looking for something a little quieter.

'Keep going further up the Lake Greg, find somewhere on the shore where's it's not so busy' said Steve, as he gawped out of the window people gazing. 'I'm with you on that', came my response.

After driving for some considerable time all of a sudden Steve told me to stop, 'here, here…pull over there on the right'. Sure enough there was a tiny layby, suitable for 2 cars….maybe 3 at a push. We jumped out and clambered down a trodden path through some trees and there we were on a deserted shoreline. It was perfect! We had an almost 360-degree panoramic view of the whole of the lake. 'Look' I said to Steve pointing to the National Trusts Steam Yacht *Gondola*, that had been ploughing her trade on these majestic waters since 1859.

'Wow, that's beautiful', said Steve, 'I think this is the spot, don't you McAttack?', he asked. 'Oh yes. It certainly is', came my reply. And with that we quickly headed off back to the car to unload and make camp for the day.

Having setup camp with our summer fold-up chairs, beach towels and 12 carrier bags, our site looked something akin to a fly tip! But Steve got some large rocks and set up the BBQ's for later.

With it being too early to eat and nothing else to do, the likely lads got changed into their swimming shorts, although before donning his swim shorts the idiot with me felt compelled to expose himself and skip up and down the rocks in his morning glory, trying vainly to alert anyone with large enough binoculars out in the Ullswater expanse that he was here is his birthday suit. Billy Connolly eat your heart out. And they'd have to have been ruddy powerful binoculars!

We then made our way gingerly to the lake. Despite it being mid-morning and already in the low 20's, the Lake was absolutely freezing! We dipped our toes in the water and squealed, it was that cold. 'I've got an idea', said Steve, 'instead of pussy-footing-around, why don't we say 1-2-3 and just dive in'?. 'Go on then', I replied, 'but let's get on with it'. And with that we waded into the lake up to our mid-riffs, 'OK. Are you ready McAttack'. Here we go. 1-2-3.......'. and with that I dived into the water. It was perishing. It was so cold it took my breath away'. When I surfaced, Steve was in bouts of hysterics and looking over his shoulder walking back to our camp, 'OY! WHERE YOU GOING' I shouted rather angrily, 'and WHY didn't you dunk into the water too you git?!' In between his mischievous bouts of laughter came the reply, 'Sod that for a game of soldiers!

Way too cold for me. I'm going to wait until after lunch when it's warmed up a little!'. 'You absolute git Redman' I shouted back at him, as he found his chair and opened up the Daily Sport for a good read.The rest of the day was amazingly relaxing. We sunbathed and watched the various boats and pleasure crafts go by and, eventually, Steve did muster the courage to join me in the Lake where we swam quite far out. After a period of time in the water the body became accustomed to the temperature. And we spent a considerable amount of the time bobbing around. It was perhaps a shame that we didn't have our own dingy, but then had we sailed off on the water we would have had to put camp McRedman back in the boot of the car, at considerable amount of time and effort! We lit one of the disposable BBQ's and cooked our lunch of sausage butties. Later in the afternoon we decided to light the other 2 disposable BBQ's and start cooking our dinner. Out of the various carrier bags I pulled out no less than 6 x boxes of regular burgers, each with 8 x beef burgers and a further 4 boxes of quarter pounder burgers, with 4 in each.

I looked at Steve. 'Did you pass your maths GCSE?' I asked, 'Errrm....yes....why you asking'. Well, you've bought 4 boxes of regular burgers'....'and?' came Steve's reply, 'well that's 32 burgers you muppet'. 'Agh....I see where you're coming from. Well, we can take them home can't we'. 'Errr....no, not really Steve. It's going to be pushing 30 degrees today and these burgers have defrosted already. I'm not sure your mums going to really want a load of rotting burgers tomorrow evening when we finally get home'. Steve looked quizzical and a bit sheepish, 'agh. Good point'. There were a few seconds silence before I continued, 'furthermore, you've bought 4 boxes of quarter pounders......that's 16 quarter pounders along with

32 regular burgers. That's 48 burgers! I know that you are always hungry but man alive....that is crazy!! And we've gotten those Chinese Steak things! And.... there's not even a soul on the shore with us here we can cook and give them to for free! You are a muppet Redman, eyes bigger than your belly'. 'Well, we won't go hungry will we McAttack', came the reply. 'NO.... we won't.... but there's a bloody food supply issue going down in Bowness today!'

So, with no point in taking anything home, and with the BBQ's being disposal ones, we cooked the lot. The food we had amassed was obscene.

We'd eaten that much meat we'd taken the Atkin's Diet to new levels. By late afternoon we had eaten so much we were fit to burst, 'I can't breathe McAttack. I feel like I do on Christmas Day'.....'that's cos you're a greedy bugger Redman. To be fair I'm also done in.'

There were at least 20 – 30 burgers charred away on the BBQ. After the course of the hour, they became burnt to a frazzle. 'Hey, let's have a skimming competition' said the Burger King himself, 'watch this' and with that he picked up a few of the black burgers and wandered a few yards to the lake where he skimmed them off the water, like you might with a flat stone. For the next 5 minutes the remaining burgers became weapons of choice for our new found skimming competition. Perhaps not the greatest of ideas but there lies the mystery of youth. And it entertained us immensely. Despite having setup Camp *McRedman* for the day and moved all our belongings from the car in a logistics operation that the Army would have been proud of, we hadn't catered for everything......no sun-cream!! As it neared 4pm the 2 of us were burnt to a cinder having spent most of the day

sunbathing. We agreed that our bodies could take no more, Steve living up to his surname and resembling a Lobster. 'Come on, we've had our fill of the day. Let's get back to Bowness, get a shower and out for a nice cold pint.
How about that', I asked Steve. 'I think you're right. Let's start getting this lot back to the car. I'll fetch some water to make sure these BBQs are out properly'. And, at not quite the same pace as whence we had arrived, we sluggishly lumbered our belonging and waste back to the car.

Once on the road we pulled over in Glenridding momentarily whilst Steve grabbed us an ice-cream each from a shop. It was even busier here than ever and the local businesses were no doubt doing a roaring trade. The ice-cream and accompanying can of pop were well received and needed on this now blistering day. Back in Bowness, once again we were fortunate enough to get parked more or less outside the B&B. The B&B was quiet, the owner and his wife nowhere to be seen. After a shower and an hour's doze, the likely lads made their way down the hill and to the Village Inn. But the consumption was rather slower than the day before and we agreed that the nightclub was most definitely not on the agenda that evening. In fact, if my memory serves me right, we went for a sit-down meal, an Italian near the B&B. But we were pretty much spent after a few hours drinking more Moosehead beer and being exposed to yet more sun.

At a sensible hour we decided to call it a night and went back to our accommodation where we slept like babies. All the same, a wonderful and memorable day. One that lives long in the memory.

The next morning, we were relatively fresh. We had decided to have a slow start and then just head back to Blackpool rather than hang around all day and risk getting caught in the traffic heading out away from the Lake District later on. We showered and made our way to the communal kitchen for breakfast together, only to find it deserted. 'Look Steve' I said, picking up a note on the table. It read roughly as follows, 'morning guys. Having to rush my wife to the hospital in Kendle as she has gone into labour. Hope you enjoyed your stay. If you wouldn't mind locking the front door and positing the key through the letter box, I'd be most grateful. No hot breakfast this morning I'm afraid but for obvious reasons. Have a safe trip home and maybe see you again'. 'Well knock me down with a feather duster', said Steve. 'Wow. That's amazing. What were the chances of that happening? How wonderful for them', I replied. And with that we had our cereal and toast breakfast.

After packing the car, we said goodbye to the lonely empty B&B and headed for home. Steve locked up whilst I turned the car around. The journey home was quiet as we listened to Seal sing some of the slower but wonderful tracks on his 1991 album. There was an air of melancholy that the weekends exploits were over and work beckoned for us both on Monday.

After an hour or so I pulled up outside Steve's house. 'Great weekend, absolutely brilliant' I said to Steve, 'yeah, absolutely spot on', he said but a little distracted as he fumbled around inside his jean pockets. 'What on earth are you doing' I asked? 'There's something digging into me and for the life of me I can't think what it is'. Steve got out of the car so he could dig deeper into his pocket and with that he pulled out a pair of keys on a key-ring. I realised what he done, 'YOU ABSOLUTE MUPPET'! It was the keys for the B&B that the owner had asked us to post back through the door once locked up. 'Oh poo', said Steve. 'Did you even lock up'? I asked, 'Yes….I definitely locked up….but then I must have put the keys in my pocket…..Oh damn….I can't believe that I did that. I'll call them tomorrow.

At least we know they aren't open for business and needing it for other customers. 'You absolute twonk. Anyway. Great weekend and enjoy work tomorrow' and, having grabbed his bag we high-fived and went our separate ways.

It was an amazing weekend with weather you could only have wished for. An adventure of youth. And always a tale to tell.

CHAPTER 7 – HEAD BANGER
Roxette – Listen to Your Heart

I had reason to reflect a little more when writing this chapter than perhaps some of the others because I think, looking back, that it was a defining moment in our lives. A point where the friendship Steve and I enjoyed really galvanised and cemented for the long-term and, in some respects, where we transitioned from youth to adulthood. It was a pivotal year in our young lives….

The year was 1991. A year I won't forget for many reasons. The Gulf-War had broken out on 17th January as the Allied Coalition reaped havoc on Saddam Hussein's own forces as part of the Dessert Storm campaign. Steve was still in the Royal Air Force at RAF Wyton and all leave was cancelled. He wrote frequently, concerned over whether he might end up in the Gulf's theatre of war. Steve was a fully qualified Chef and had trained at the RAF's Catering College in Aldershot and one might assume he was in a trade largely unaffected by a distant war.

But regardless of trade or armed force, one was in harm's way in that region and bases such as Dhahran in Saudi Arabia and Bahrain were often under Scud Missile attack by Iraqi. Siren warnings were a frequent occurrence as Patriot missile systems worked hard to take out the threat. That certainly focussed Steve's mind on life and the virtues of being part of the armed forces.

I remember the 17th January vividly. I'd just been to the Police training college at Hutton for some exams (against my desire to be honest) and my dad had driven me there. On the way home, not long out of Hutton, the news broke on the car Radio. We pulled over into a layby to listen. It was definitely an *Oh My God* moment as it was the first military conflict for Britain since the Falklands war in 1982. Over the years I have read a lot about the air war in Iraqi during 1991 [Gulf War I]. Who knew that before I got up for breakfast that morning Squadron Leader Emilio Mason was screaming across the Saudi desert leading his Tornado Fighter Jet formation into an Iraqi target. Another reason it was a memorable year is that I started working in Her Majesty's Civil Service on the 25th February. My first career and one that lasted nearly 17 years and one I enjoyed very much.

And so it was that in the prime of our youth, with the world at our feet and with the threat of going to war behind Steve, at least for the time being, I suggested that we book a holiday abroad. Just the two of us. A boy's jolly holiday in the sun. I think it's fair to say that he didn't need asking twice! It would be the first holiday abroad either of us had arranged without our respective families. FREEDOM!!

Back in 1991 there was no internet for searching holiday deals – although I think Tim Berners-Lee's invention was up and running for the pioneering few! Instead, I limited my holiday searching to Ceefax, a Teletext service obtained through your TV that advertised holidays. It was incredibly basic.....but it worked. Eventually I found a good hotel called Las Piramides in Tenerife's Playa de las Americas resort.

It sounded superb and we weren't disappointed when we finally got there. Steve was still in the RAF based at Wyton in Cambridgeshire, so he posted money home to pay for the holiday and spending money to his family in Cleveleys.

Two weeks in the sun. Just the two of us and a pocket load of spending money. We couldn't wait and knew this was going to be the ultimate adventure. We'd booked the holiday months in advance so we had, what felt like, an interminable wait. The days and hours just couldn't go quick enough for either of us and the days seemed to drag - Steve being located down in Cambridgeshire and myself at the Civil Service site in Norcross near Blackpool. Steve was preparing meals, sometimes banquets and sophisticated dining-in nights for the Officers Mess, with Guard Duties on certain evenings and a field catering deployment to the Highlands of Scotland, all part and parcel of his duties.

Meanwhile yours truly was processing Attendance Allowance claims and taking calls from the general public (no formal helplines in those days), but I was making money and happy enough.
There was also a superb social scene with the team I was working with. Good memories and thoroughly decent people, which is important to me in life.

After months and months of waiting the day arrived, although it was nip and tuck for Steve. I can't recall how many trains he had to catch to get to the Poulton-Le-Fylde station not far from his parents' home in Cleveleys, but it was a lot. Huntingdon, Peterborough, Leeds, Preston then Poulton-Le-Fylde. An exhausting day spent on British Rails services.....British Rail wasn't privatised until 1994! But he made it home, albeit around midnight. Too late for a beer, a shame but at least we were fresh for the taxi service the next morning, which Steve's Dad had kindly arranged for us.

The next day arrived and I had my case out at the front of my Parents house on Warbreck Hill Road in the small hours. I'd said my goodbyes to my parents and siblings the night before given the ridiculously early pick-up. I'd been read the riot act from my parents about being careful, doing nothing stupid and the usual conversation around if you get into trouble with the Spanish Police then they'll lock you up and throw away the key. Oh….and they'll wrap you in a rug and beat you to a pulp. Nice. What could go wrong?
I was going to a foreign country with Steve for 2 weeks in the sun. As Steve always said, Trust Me…I'm Your Best Mate'! Then again……

I was so eager to go I stood out on the street waiting for Steve to arrive. I can't remember the date but I believe it was late July. It was going to be a stunning summers day in Blackpool. It was already light and the dawn chorus was in full swing. But it was eerily silent. The world was asleep and there was no traffic whatsoever on the road. I'm a morning person, always have been and Steve the nightbird. Funny. We both liked this time in the morning….but from opposite ends of the spectrum, for myself getting up, for Steve the party usually just coming to an end!
A taxi, with its sidelights on, came into view…the only car on the road. It was Steve for sure and the excitement was now palpable. We'd agreed that he should be picked up first as my parents' house was closer to the M55 Motorway. The car drew up and stopped. The door flung open, 'Yo…..you ready to P.A.R.T.Y?' came the yell from one excited passenger, 'Hell Yeah' came my reply. And with my suitcase in the boot of the taxi we set off to Manchester Airport…….but not before the taxi driver insisted on seeing both our passports and *paper*

airline tickets. Perhaps he had us down as the Likely Lads or maybe he'd just been on too many wild goose chases in the past with youngsters? Either way we were good and hit the road busting with excitement.

Manchester Airport was waiting for us along with the now long-gone Britannia Airways, which included their new Boeing 767 widebody aircraft. And nobody paid extra for an inflight meal in those days. Everybody got one. All the Airline stewardesses were stunning (and Stewards I'm sure), the drinks were free, the inflight movie worked and all was well with the world. When I look back, I see 2 decent lads. We had been brought up well, and despite our tales of daring do we never shamed our families, never gotten into fights nor caused trouble or touched drugs. We always knew how to enjoy ourselves to the max – our lives were anything but vanilla – and a belly laugh was had every time we teamed up. Always, without fail. But we knew where the line was, which unfortunately some young people don't. I truly believe that our Air Training Corps (ATC) discipline had much to do with that. Work hard, play hard – a cliché but true.

Our Britannia Airways jet landed safely at Reina Sofia Airport and two expectant lads from the Fylde Coast waited impatiently to disembark the aircraft. What fun awaited? What might we get up to? Who might we meet? Well, I'm going to tell you......are you ready?

As with all good package holidays right up until the 2000's a holiday representative was there to greet the lemmings off the plane and escort them to their allotted coach for the transfer to their chosen resort hotel. This was always followed by the obligatory talk enroute from the resort representative using the coach microphone, who was usually a blonde sort from Basildon or Guilford, who proceeded to explain, for the uneducated British traveller, that you can't drink the tap water, don't pay more than 1 Peseta for a pint in the bars and the Dog and Partridge sold the best Sunday Roast in town! Yep, the €euro still hadn't arrived and wouldn't do until 1999. The dull and rather awkward speeches were always concluded with information on the next morning's welcome briefing in the hotel foyer and a final reminder for everyone to kindly tip Manuel the Coach driver who was a superb driver but had 16 kids and a wife to feed. Always a blessing when it ended.

As it happens the Airport wasn't too far away and we were one of the first hotel drops. Eventually we pulled up outside the Las Piramides Hotel, which was made up of 2 main buildings . Despite the fact we had jointly agreed on this hotel the penny had only just dropped, 'Agh….now I see why it's called Las Piramides, the buildings are like Pyramids', I said aloud, 'Oh yeah' said Steve with an air of surprise. The other people on the coach must have thought Bill and Ted were on their most excellent adventure!

So, with our new pull along suitcases, Bermuda shorts and bum-bags, which were all the rage back then, we triumphantly made our way into the Hotel Reception. Check-in was easy enough and our passports were confiscated for 24hrs whilst we were registered with the local Police, which was standard practice back then. We quickly found our Apartment, which was really pretty decent with a double bed each in our own bedrooms, a huge living room area, kitchen and balcony. Not much of a view from the balcony to be honest, but we were never going to be in, so we really weren't too bothered.

Being sensible chaps, we decided to have a walk around the hotel before unpacking to familiarise ourselves with our surroundings and to also stock up with the provisions for the week. Namely 5litres of water, milk, tea, coffee, bread, butter, cheese/jam and as much beer and crisps as we could carry.

Having unpacked and changed we cracked open a beer and sat out on the balcony in the hot evening air. It was now around 7:00pm and the light had faded, the hotel and surroundings taking on a new feel. As we looked away to our right we could see neon lights not too far in the distance, indicating where there might be some nightlife. 'Here's to a fab holiday McAttack' said Steve crunching his can of beer against my own, 'I'll drink to that. Bottoms-up old chap', I replied. You just can't beat that first beer on holiday. The one after you've unpacked and are showered and ready for your first evening out. The hassle of the journey finally behind you and that thought of 2-weeks with no work, just total freedom and good times.

After we'd finished our beers, we headed off towards the bright lights or, as they are called in every British Tourist destination across Europe *'the strip'*, better known as Veronicas.

We found a rather nice-looking Pizzeria enroute and gorged ourselves on a wonderful Pizza along with more beer. Having enjoyed our evening meal, we headed on down to the strip in Playa de las Americas.

Back in 1991 Veronicas, was mainly contained to a huge rectangular building block that had 2 floors, with umpteen bars and nightclubs. Adjacent to this block on the other side of the road were more bars, which tended to be a little quieter because geographically they weren't in the sweet spot (location, location, location). But their drink prices were not as high, which worked for us! As we were to find out, the strip was a rather mental place and anything could and did happen....

On approaching *the strip* we noted that, as luck would have it, the bar nearest us was lit up like a Christmas Tree with flashing lights. It looked pretty cool and we were straight into this bar like a flash! It was called *Rags Bar* and, given we'd be there for a fortnight we considered it rude not to try each bar in turn, so Rags was our starting point. Rags Bar was great. It had neon lighting everywhere and the ultraviolet lighting made anything white glow. It also made your suntan look tan-tastic.....once you had one! Also, unlike some of the other bars, it was fully air conditioned, which for us Brits was a luxury. It was fantastic to cool off in there after a blazing hot day on the beach. However, that first night was a bit of a disaster though owing to the fact that when it came to alcohol we were complete novices. We knew about beer but not much else. The likely lads made their way to the bar, 'righty-O-John, what have you got on your happy hour special tonight then' asked Steve of the Spanish barman. 'Hi guys, my name is Emilio. Great to see you. You guys just arrive, where you from?' asked the young barman with much gusto and who was barely older than ourselves. 'Agh, great to meet you, Emilio! Well, we've just landed and come from Manchester, here for 2-weeks...and you're the lucky one to serve us first', said Steve, 'We're from near Manchester.....a place called Blackpool' I qualified. 'Agh very nice. Well, you will have a good time here. We have all drinks. Happy hour until 8pm every day. You be happy. Pina Colada buy 1 get 3 free....very special offer'. I twigged straight away, 'so Emilio, it's not yet 8pm, so if we buy a Pina Colada, we get 4 each?'. Emilio smiled, 'si, very special offer for you guys. You want this? asked the waiter smiling. Steve and myself looked at each other as if in disbelief....quantity was definitely the winner here, no matter what Pina Colada was! 'Hell yeah', said Steve with aplomb, 'cheap as chips' I said laughing. And sure enough the barman had no less than 8 Pina Colada's lined up in front of us in no time, albeit in cheap white plastic cups.

Now, there will be many of you reading this that have the wisdom of many years on your side and already know, before reading too much further, that this isn't going to end well. Approximately 4 lagers, a pepperoni Pizza and 4 Pina Colada's *down-the-*hatch before we've even got beyond the first bar is not exactly a great mix. In case you don't know, Pina Colada is a cocktail made with rum, cream of coconut or coconut milk and pineapple juice, usually served either blended or shaken with ice, garnished with either a pineapple wedge, maraschino cherry, or both. What a right pair of tarts we must have looked......or plonkers. And it was disgusting. Despite neither of us liking it we consumed the lot. It took us a fair while, and as the bar began to get busy, we took a few strange looks but we were now properly getting sozzled....and grimacing with each mouthful.

After 45 minutes slurping this cocktail Steve suggested we go and recce the rest of the strip. We bade our farewell to Emilio and literally fell out of the bar, knocking a plastic chair sideways in the process. We we're bladdered and the night hadn't even got going.

We ventured down the strip, which was now a blaze of neon lights the day having turned to night. Predominately

British touts intercepted unsuspecting punters, trying to drag you into *their* bar with the offer of free drinks and happy hour, 'where you from lads, fancy a free drink, best place in Tenerife'…..and so it went on. Bar after bar and more and more alcohol we guzzled. One English lad from the north west of England badgered us every single day….and every day we said that we would come to his bar before the end of the holiday and attend his organised pub-crawl. He reminded us each time we saw him, 'don't forget lads….you're mine on your last night'. What a memory that guy had.

A few hours evaporated – how does that happen when you're on a pub crawl, that feeling you've only been out for 30minutes but 4hrs has elapsed (?) – and now feeling tired from the days travel and somewhat inebriated I ventured to Steve that we curtail our first night, 'Steve, first night and all that, why don't we venture back towards our hotel, there were a few bars over there'. Steve didn't need too much convincing, 'roger that….feeling a little ropey to be honest' replied Steve. And with that we headed off back towards our hotel, dodging all the amazing offers that were coming our way.

Eventually the raucous sound of the strip dissipated behind us and we came to a more family & couple orientated part of town, many bars with soft comfy chairs and mediocre cabaret style entertainment. We continued past these at which point Steve said, 'hey…..let's go in this one' and without batting an eyelid I followed saying 'hola' to the Spanish doorman on the way in.

It was a strange bar because you had to go down a very steep set of stairs and through some red double doors at the bottom. But once through the doors it was a big spacious nightclub with dancefloor and a fair few people in. The air conditioning was working a treat although the Pina-colada concoction was still floating around in our bellies. 'Here' said Steve passing me some Pesetas, 'you fire a beer in as I'm needing the toilet big time….feeling a bit dicky', 'Yeah…no worries', dicky meaning it was the sort of toilet problem you definitely didn't want on a night out!

Steve disappeared and I sat alone at the bar and ordered in a couple of cerveza's. He was gone a long time, I'm not so sure the pizza and concoction of booze was mixing very well. But I wasn't alone for long. A Spanish lady in a very bright Lycra dress and not much else came over and started smiling at me whilst she played with the straw in her drink. 'Hello' I ventured, 'just arrived from England', 'very nice' she said in broken English, continuing to smile. 'You work here then' I asked, she laughed, 'si', 'agh very good……nice hot weather eh', 'si…you like it hot…..I like it hot too', 'yes, only rain in Cleveleys', 'si……you come, we have fun in the sun', said the bronzed lady with a broad smile. She then started to run her incredibly long painted finger nails up and down my right arm, 'you funny… nice guy'. I was well chuffed, 'agh, thanks, very decent of you. You're very friendly' I replied. 'I come back here, un minuto' as she shuffled off towards the toilets in her high heels. Blimey, what a first night I thought to myself.

At this point Steve reappeared, 'eh up mucker, did you fire them beers in'?, 'I sure did, here you go pal' I said passing Steve his ice-cold beer. 'Hey, I've only gone and pulled and we're on our first night! I've had this right sort over wearing nothing but a tea-cosy, rubbing my arm and telling me how wonderful I am. Bit old maybe…..but I ain't complaining' I said to Steve triumphantly. Steve threw a huge cheesy smile, 'you absolute dipstick. You complete and utter dipstick', came his rebuke.

'Oh, charming….getting jealous again are we?' I replied. 'No. I ain't jealous you dipstick.
Have a look around this bar. Open your eyes and tell me what you see,' said Steve. I hadn't really taken in the other people around the bar, but now looking it became clear that there were a lot of couples! 'Blimey…..it's a couples bar……..maybe she's off to get her fella'. Steve was nearly on the floor laughing, 'you are a complete muppet.

It's not a couple's bar….sweet Jesus….you really have no idea do you? Let's just say ALL the ladies are working in here'. I gulped, the penny had dropped, 'OMG…….you've brought me into a house of ill repute!'. Steve was beside himself laughing, 'come on McAttack……let's drink up before she comes back and starts rubbing your other arm…..she's a bit of a horror bag anyway'. We both laughed, supped up and beat it back to the hotel for a nightcap. It had been a very long day and our recce down the strip had been enough for one night.

Day 1 was behind us. I guess I could write about all the various shenanigans that went on day-by-day, but that would fill a book in itself and, in any case, my memory is a little hazy…..either that or we were so drunk most of the time it's not particularly clear what happened anyway!

Instead, I shall remind myself of a few memorable flashbacks from that balmy fortnight in the sun.

First off, I remember the water sports, which featured mostly in week 1….probably because we had a pocket full of money and, as at the start of any holiday, we were flush with cash. Banana boats, ringo's, jet skis and paragliding were all enjoyed. We also had a boat trip excursion with drinks onboard. In addition, we had an organised trip to the waterpark, where we had a brilliant time but managed to get burnt to death and left the water park looking like a pair of lobsters. It's fair to say we lived life to the full. Steve and myself always got on. Never a cross word said or bad thought. We were having the time of our lives. Looking back, there was something magical about this trip.

About 3 days into the holiday and we came upon some other bars a little bit more upmarket. They were much more sophisticated and had bar prices to match, almost treble that of the strip. But it was nice to go somewhere different. I have to tell this story here because I know Steve harps on about it and will kill me if I don't include. At the time it passed me by a little, but certainly not Steve! We had gone into BOSS Bar, complete with flaming stands and trendy furnishings.
The Mafia would have felt quite comfortable here....maybe they did?! It was pretty empty though as it was early on in the evening when we arrived there.

There was a very attractive Spanish lady behind the bar and, whilst perhaps several years older than the pair of us, cupid had smacked Steve so hard he was completely love struck…..totally poleaxed. I wasn't there when he met his wife Ellen the first time many years later, but I can only assume it was the same. Steve was so mesmerised by this beauty that it was like he entered another world. There was some serious flirting going on from both parties……their corresponding understanding of one another's languages was pretty much non-existent, but the language of love was talking right enough! I found it all very cringeworthy and uncomfortable as the gooseberry watching on so sat at a distance and sipped my ice-cold beer. However, the sentinel moment arrived when said exotic lady poured some fresh cream, that was going in a cocktail for Steve, accidentally over her fingers and then into her mouth in a particularly suggestive manner. I think it's fair to say Steve crumpled on the spot. The poor lad almost collapsed. He was a quivering wreck. Never seen before or again since. I had to drag the poor boy out of there in a mesmerised trance like state!

On approximately night 3 it was Greg's turn to impress. I had befriended a group of Belgian's, the eldest of the group being a lovely blonde girl who was the same age as myself. She looked the proper 1980's rock queen. Big shoulder pads, huge blond perm.....she was from Europe and could easily have been in the rock-band of the same name! I liked her a lot. She was lovely and we went on a couple of holiday dates, but nothing serious. I always recall that they lived in the north of Belgium and spoke Flemish. Steve privately derided her all week calling her Heidi from the mountains.....girlfriend sabotage strikes again! But soon enough she and her Belgian pals were off back to Brussels. Steve's lack of support for Anglo-Belgian relations had been noted!

Approximately half way through the holiday and after way too much sun and way too much booze we decided to have an Arab evening. I have absolutely no recollection of how this started or why, but our Bermuda shorts, vests and bumbags were dropped in favour of nothing more than a white bed sheet draped around us. The Arab look was finished off by putting red and white chequered tea-towels over our heads held on tightly with black shoe laces and the eastern promise look finished with a pair of shades.

I'm not sure what reaction we got but clearly we thought this was humorous and we paraded around the hotel and then off down the street for a few beers. I'm sure people either thought we were a) off to a fancy-dress party... or b) mental. Again, we had fun and I suppose that's all that matters.

Around the same time, part way through the holiday we bumped into 2 sisters from a town not too far from Blackpool. They were friendly enough but I'm not sure that Steve's charm offensive landed particularly well, 'Yes....I'm a fully qualified Chef in the Royal Air Force....I regularly do Officers Balls....'. Either way they agreed to a dinner date.....and we were cooking! I had a feeling this didn't bode well given the rubbish 2 iron rings in the poxy kitchen and the lack of decent ingredients available in the local super-mercado. However, Steve insisted on impressing the ladies, so instead of sunbathing or jet-skiing we were off to the shops! We purchased so much ingredients that it would have been cheaper to take them out for a slap-up meal in a local restaurant! Steve spent the whole afternoon making a rue (a sauce base for the dish he was making) which was a disaster and looked like glue or the web material Spiderman shoots out of his wrists. The meal was a shocker, the ladies were pretty unimpressed and shall we say the night was a bit of a failure.

The Lord loves a trier. The ladies in question lived directly downstairs from our apartment and shortly after leaving the next morning we could hear a bit of a ding-dong going on. The walls, floors and ceilings in Spanish property aren't usually much more than breeze block and we could nearly make out their argument. We therefore got a glass cup each from the bathroom and laid on the floor with one ear to the glass and then held our breath '1-2-3' so as to hear. It did the trick and we could just about hear their conversation.....which turned out to be pretty dull. All the same, it was fun for spies like us!

The week wore on and more and more people, whether they be holiday makers, bar staff or holiday reps, got to know the likely lads and 'where the party was at'. We literally couldn't walk in any bar or restaurant without someone shouting us over. We made an impact and we felt loved where ever we went. I'd spent many a morning on my own though, in the swimming pool or out for breakfast whilst Steve nursed his hangover and, as we know, Steve requires precisely 13hrs sleep before he's ready to go again......12hrs 59minutes is not enough. But I'd enjoyed those quiet moments on my own.

I recall walking along the beach, thinking how strange so many old people were out at this early hour, many swimming in the sea. How the younger generation were mangled each night and missed this special part of the day. But mangled or not, I always love the mornings and that freshness each day. I watched a tall German fellow, maybe in his early seventies and he stood proudly looking out to sea, hands on hip deciding maybe whether to wade in. I contemplated that he would be long dead by the time I reached his age and I wondered what might happen in my life between now and me reaching his age? Would I be stood there on that beach or any other beach across the world, on a beautiful sunny morning reflecting on a life gone by. I was sure I would be. But for now, I had to think ahead to our last day and night in Tenerife.

Our last evening out was, to put it mildly, rather mental and shall never be forgotten. The day prior to the last night Steve had blagged it with the English lad called John, running the organised pub crawls, whom we'd met at the very start of the holiday and side-lined every night, that if we brought 20 people then we could have free drinks in all the bars.

He agreed….but didn't believe that we could do that. Steve did this for 3 reasons i) because he likes a challenge, ii) because he wanted to show how popular we were and iii) because we were nearly skint after living it up for a fortnight. To be truthful the 3rd reason was probably the only reason!

We got freshened up and togged up in our best party clothes for the big night out. I don't recall eating but I suspect it was a cheap burger as we really were nearly out of money and it was Traveller's cheques in those days, no ATM machines or debit cards!! We had told anyone and everyone we had met to come on the Pub crawl and, at 8pm we arrived at the agreed meeting spot. We were not disappointed. Looking back, I can see the queue now and there must have been 30 people along with other punters that the lad had brought in himself. He was delighted and so were we as he held his word and we were on free ale all evening! Top bloke!!

And off we set with the entourage behind us. Steve was in absolutely top form and the gags were flying left right and centre. Bar after bar there were huge cries of 'whoooooooa……salud' as nasty cocktails and beers were consumed.

Before we knew it Steve and myself also had a girl each on our arm. No idea how but it just happened . They were the same age as us and from Bournemouth. And so the party went on into overdrive. We were like one long drunken chain gang, going to bar after bar……places Steve and I had never frequented during the fortnight we'd been there. In addition to the free drinks from the Pub crawl organizer many of our holiday friends were lining them up for us. It was starting to get really messy and was late…..perhaps 1am. I recall vaguely being in a nightclub, everyone dancing and the unisex toilet having no door? What a dump. There were now more and more people joining us and it was unclear if the pub crawl had finished as it had become one giant mass of people getting wrecked.

Around 2:30am I became aware that I had lost Steve, but I still seemed to have my quota from the Pub Crawl, maybe 10 people. It was really rather bizarre. I think we'd all given up on the Pub Crawl but these random people whom I barely knew were following me like a tour guide. I also still had one of the girls from Bournemouth on my arm who had taken a shine, it was like we were on a formal date! I recall turning to the motley crew in tow, 'look…..I've lost my pal….I need to find him….if you want to follow me then no problem'. It was a poor attempt to lose them. It didn't work.

We looked high and low. There were bars at street level and at a higher level that you reached by going up some stairs. I had nearly given up looking for Steve, but now starting to sober up I was growing a little concerned for him. Over the fortnight we'd never separated on a night out – safety together and all that. I'd also seen the worst of Steve and booze on a night out in Blackpool where he'd endangered himself. Furthermore, we had an early bus collection in the morning to take us to the Airport for our Britannia Airways service home to the UK. I had to find him.

We had covered nearly all the bars when we decided to go down the far side of the upper level…still with the remnants of the pub crawl party following me. As we neared a grey coloured bar with brown windows, I could see that it was absolutely rammed to the gunnels. There was standing room only.

It was like a scene out of an Asterix comic, with folk squashed against the windows it was that busy. And they were all cheering '10, 9, 8, 7, 6, 5, 4, 3, 2, 1.....Wooooooooah....Head Bangeeeeeeeerrrrrrrrr!!!'.   As I drew level with the door, which had two very large doormen, I spotted Steve, 'LOOK!' I exclaimed to my followers in disbelief, 'there's Steve!!'.

And there before me was a scene I shall never forget to the day I die. There must have been 400 people crammed into this bar and up on the stage was a huge Throne. Directly behind the Throne's headrest was a huge bullseye target. 'What on earth....' I muttered aloud, my jaw dropping open as I watched Steve, complete with Eddie the Eagle style crappy helmet and superman cape, put his head back and open his mouth wide. A barman then poured a ridiculous amount of cheap Spanish liquor into his mouth and told Steve to hold his nose. The Barman then turned to the crowd, a good mix of age groups assembled here from all corners of Europe to watch this nutter! The countdown started again, '10, 9, 8, 7, 6, 5, 4, 3, 2, 1.....Wooooooooah....Head Bangeeeeeeeerrrrrrrrr!!!' the crowd roared and, right on cue, the barman slammed Steve's head into the target right behind him with such force that the liquor slammer went straight down his cake-hole. The crowd roared with delight and cries of 'crazy English guy' could be heard from somewhere in the crammed bar.

Never in my life had I ever seen anything like this! The crowd went mental, 'more, more, more'. I was worried this crowd were going to kill my best pal, but there was no way through the crowd. The posse behind me had melded into the fierce audience in front of me.

By a stroke of good fortune John, the English Lad who had arranged the Pub Crawl, was standing near the door and happened to look towards me, 'mental your pal is, completely mental' he said smiling with glee. 'Yeah, I know, thought I'd lost him for the night. What on earth is he doing', I said with concern. 'Don't worry I'll keep an eye on him,' said John.

It was now very late, around 4:30am. I don't know what came over me but I turned to the young lady on my arm, 'say, have you ever watched the sun rise over the Atlantic', 'no....but I'd like to' came the reply. Bingo. I turned to John, 'can you tell that muppet that I'll be down on the beach and don't let him leave without me'. John winked, 'of course pal. I'll make sure that he finds you!

And off I went with a beautiful girl to watch the sun rise over the Atlantic. We watched the night slip away as the new day started to break....but alas my geography proved to be rubbish as the sun rises in the east and the Beach was west facing....hence it rose directly behind us! I then plucked up even more courage, 'I've never been skinny dipping before either' and in order to seize the moment the two intrepid strangers removed their clothing and ran into the sea naked, swimming out a short distance. Quite a surreal and pleasant experience I must say. We looked back towards the town, the neon lights starting to be switched off and the day finally breaking. We bobbed around in the water, contemplating life. It was magic.

But then my horrors of all horrors. I saw 3 or 4 figures staggering onto the beach, one of them was John and........I didn't have to wait long to figure out who else was there.....'now then...now then.......what have we got here' came a very, very drunken familiar voice. 'Oh......we have been a naughty boy haven't we Greggy', came the mischievous laugh. 'Oh.....what have we here.....I think these are your clothes if I'm not mistaken……..I'll look after them for you….'. I was fuming and waded out of the water as fast as I could, using my hands to shield the place where the sun doesn't shine. 'Steve…..give me back my clothes' I demanded. But Steve was totally bladdered and acting stupidly, 'Not until you say pretty, please…..you'll get them back at some point, trust me I'm your best mate'. Nightmare scenario. I ran at Steve but he ran off towards the path leading off the beach, whilst John and the other 2 random blokes laughed their socks off. The lady whom I was with had managed to get her own clothing and disappeared…never to be seen again…ever! Girlfriend sabotage once again!!

Now I became aware that there were families with young kids coming on to the beach…with Lilo's and buckets and spades in hand. What a nightmare, 'give me my clothes….given me my clothes' I demanded as I chased Steve all over the beach and the promenade. This went on for 10 minutes and it was only a matter of time before the Spanish Bill turned up and we got arrested.

However, things came to an abrupt end. Steve looked knackered, like he was having a coronary and panting for breath calling time, 'I think……me old mucker……that we finished the holiday in style…….don't you'? He asked almost sober. I took my clothes off him and popped them on, 'I think we did pal' followed by a high 5. We said our farewell to John and company and made our way back to the hotel. It must have been 7am as we staggered home happy as Larry…….and shattered.

We grabbed 2 or 3 hours sleep before it was time to get up and ready to leave. We'd packed our suitcases the night before so that was one less thing to worry about. I woke Steve who was in a right mess, 'Steve….Steve…' trying to wake him from his unconscious mess, 'Steve…..we're getting collected in an hour….time to get showered'. I had already showered and packed my remaining items. 'Water….I need water….I'm dehydrated' said Steve in a muffled drunken manner, 'I've got no money Steve….I'm completely skint, zilch'. Steve managed to speak, 'I've got some in my wallet….but that's all I've got…get water and something else'. I took the money…… it wasn't a lot…and then I went and did something stupid. By something else Steve meant food. Our flight was around 6pm in the evening, which meant an in-flight food service at 7pm…….which meant we would be without food for a long time. But, I'm ashamed to say, yours truly totally bombed out.

I went to the Supermarket and bought a reasonably large bottle of Highland Spring water….but that was it. The money was gone. When I got back to our hotel room Steve took the bottle from me and began gulping it down, his mouth was clearly like the Sahara Dessert, 'what else did you get' he asked, looking terrible. 'That's all I could get with the money', Steve looked at the bottle label then back at me, 'you absolute dimwit. You can get the local aqua for next to nothing and you go and get imported Highland Spring…….which is more expensive than beer over here! You absolute muppet…..we've nothing now for the rest of the day and we're hungover to buggery'.

And he was right. We might as well have been dumped in the dessert. We were desperately thirty and hungry for the rest of the day. The coach eventually picked us up and took us on our way to the Airport, where there was a water fountain that we gulped from. By the time we got to board the flight we were incredibly hungry, thirsty and still hungover.

We had to sit in the middle section of the widebody Boeing 767 and, shortly after take-off, endure the torture of smelling the food being warmed in the galley. We were like the Bisto Kids…..we were desperate for food! An old couple next to us could see us salivating! 'We've had nothing all day….we're Hank Marvin' we said in unison….we probably stank of stale ale too!

Eventually the food came and we couldn't rip the cover off quick enough. The starter was egg mayonnaise, 'you hate mayonnaise McAttack…..can I have it?'……'No…..I'll eat anything tonight' I replied and sure enough I did! Embarrassingly I'd clocked that the elderly couple next to us had no appetite for either their starter nor bread rolls, 'do you mind' I said glancing at the food ready to go to waste, 'No… help yourself son', with a wry smile etched across their faces. What a sight we must have been! After eating the boys from Blackpool were zonked-out and slept like babies for the remainder of the flight back to Manchester.

Eventually, the likely lads landed home in blighty to be greeted by the rain and our parents and the inevitable Spanish Inquisition,' did you have a nice relaxing time', 'I hope you both behaved yourselves?', 'you've got a nice tan Greg, why haven't you Steve', 'Did you get on…..are you still best mates', 'I hope you didn't drink too much'……

If only they knew……..we'd had the time of our lives!

CHAPTER 8 – WESTMORLAND AVE FIREWORK DISPLAY
Bon Jovi – Blood on Blood

Through the years there were more social gatherings at Westmorland Avenue Cleveleys than I care to remember. They were always welcoming and always raucous! Steve's parents, Bill and Val knew how to host a party and entertain. There was an inevitability of Bill getting his guitar out well into the evening for the obligatory singalong. I never told him when he was alive, but I loved those nights. There is something treasured about watching someone talented play and sing and encourage audience participation. Indeed, Bill had played in a local band during the 1960's called *Ready Steady Go* and played at venues such as the Merry England Bar on Blackpool's North Pier. Val had been a *groupie* and they shared the same taste in music. I remember Bill showing me a few basic chords one evening and us both singing Dream by the Everly Brothers with the rest of the family and friends joining in. Pure magic.

Aside from the usual get together for birthdays, a key highlight each year was Bonfire Night. This usually lasted 2 nights for myself with a gathering for my own family in Blackpool on one evening and another gathering at Steve's the next. I enjoyed both immensely. But I shall focus on one particular evening at the Westmorland Avenue Firework Display that shall long be remembered. Before going on any further I should point out that the nanny state in which we now live has ensured that such stories cannot be repeated and told in the future. Probably just as well but rather dull and drab all the same. Health and Safety was a new buzz word in the late 1980s and something that happened at your dad's place of work, not necessarily in the real world where people lived and played! So, be warned, this chapter carries a *'do not try this at home'* banner!

The day in question arrived, bonfire night! Steve's parents, Bill and Val, were having a bit of a shindig (party) and putting a spread on…….more commonly referred to as a buffet! And, as Bill would say, 'they were grand as out'….and they damn well were!
On arriving at Westmorland Avenue, I knocked on the door and was let in by Steve, 'come on in McAttack' said Steve in a lively manner. The house was a throng of people, friends and family, pretty much all of whom I knew. Steve's house was a traditional semi-detached property and was usually rammed to the gunnels on nights like these.

The party was already alive and kicking with loud chatter, laughter and music blaring from the Stereo System in the back room. As per usual at any party, the kitchen was the epicentre of 'the do'……..it was also where the booze was and the bottle opener! Perhaps unusually, even for that time, Steve's mum had opted to install a coal fired boiler system, brought from a previous house they lived at. And I could see why. There is nothing like a coal fire and the warmth that it radiates throughout the kitchen and beyond into the rest of the house.

I patted the family dog Tina on the head, who must be said was sure for some good titbits on a night like this! I grabbed a beer, said a brief hello to a few of Steve's family and friends, gave his Mum the continental style kiss on each cheek and went into the back-room where Steve had gone ahead of me. It was open plan, no door, so the rabble and noise from the kitchen continued unabated. As usual, the dining table had been pushed to one side and *the spread* covered in clingfilm and tinfoil, ready to be unravelled at the allotted time, which was usually around 9pm. As Bill often told me, 'you can have a good drink then a good eat, but you can't have a good eat then a good drink'. How true.

So, the plan was for much merriment for the next 2 hours, whilst letting off fireworks and then, after the frivolity and excitement of live fireworks, everyone would get stuck into the buffet.

Steve waved me over to a corner near the French patio windows where a ridiculous amount of pyrotechnics had been assembled. Some of these had been brought by other family and friends but, as you will have found elsewhere in this book, Steve is habitually inclined to out-do yours truly, and the stack and associated cost incrementally rose year-on-year. 'hey, Look at this little lot, what you think', said Steve with a grin more suited to a Cheshire Cat! I had to admit, the Redman's had outdone themselves this year and we were in for a beano! Even better, after years of Bill insisting that he let the fireworks off, this year he had entrusted Steve, his brother Neil and myself to do the annual display.

He must have banged his head or been drunk.....either way it made for an interesting evening! I looked over the pyrotechnic booty. I always think that the marketing team at firework companies do such a great job. Steve, Neil and myself riffled through each box, all you could hear was 'wow.... look at this one...*Cataclysmic Explosion*.....yes please sir'.
We were kids in a sweet shop. Spectacular as they were, it wouldn't take long to send £150 worth of refined pig manure into the Cleveleys night sky! Nonetheless, how fantastic and

none of us could wait.

As in every tale to tell in this book there is a twist. As Neil slipped into the kitchen to fetch another drink, Steve shepherded me outside to an adjacent outhouse. As per usual Steve had a surprise up his sleeve. Noone else at the party had seen us disappear. Steve lent over between a deep freezer and some fishing equipment and pulled out a rocket the size of which wouldn't have looked out of place in her majesty's arsenal! My jaw dropped, 'what the....' I gasped, 'yes.... just what I thought when I got it...what a beauty eh. We'll save this bugger until last.... don't tell my mum and dad though, nobody knows I've got it ok'. The rocket was enormous and Steve literally had to cradle it like a baby. It was *public display standard* and surely not something he should have acquired. It had a cylindrical body but with a huge ball on the top the size of a small football. The traditional stick used to launch such rockets wasn't a stick put rather a plank of wood. To be frank I had NEVER seen anything like it. 'Where the hell did you get that', I asked mesmerised, 'ask no questions and I'll tell you no lies' came the reply from Steve, a phrase I'd heard more than once before.

Steve held the ordnance out, 'here, see what you think'. I took the giant firework with a little trepidation, 'blimey, its heavy' I said, rather taken aback by its weight and fearing just how much high explosive might be in it. Unlike the *family* box of fireworks in the house that the marketing men had done such a great job on, this firework was devoid of any such colourful packaging or exotic name.

This was a serious piece of pyrotechnic and clearly something entrusted to a professional display team. I noticed a warning sign on the side, which I read out aloud, 'NOT TO BE USED

IN A PLACE LESS THAN 400 SQUARE METERS!'. There was a momentary silence as we looked at each other, 'flipping eck Steve, I don't think your mum and dads garden is that big.....it's more like 40 metres squared.... not 400!'. Steve smiled, 'blah.....sod that.... we'll be right.... trust me...I'm your best mate.....'. 'I'd seen those mischievous eyes a hundred times before and knew nothing was going to change his mind about letting this enormous firework off. 'We'll wait until the party has died off a little and everyone has gone indoors, then we'll see how good it is', said Steve with relish. With that said the missile was once again hidden down the side of the cabinet freezer and off we trotted back to the party, which judging from the racket was in full swing.

'Ladies and Gentlemen.....it you would like to make your way into the garden the Westmorland Avenue Firework Display is about to commence', boomed Steve with cupped hands through the kitchen so everyone could hear. There were cheers and whoops as the intoxicated gang of about 20 people gathered near the patio doors, now with jackets donned but still clutching their drinks. Steve, Neil and myself had lit our tappers and grabbed various fireworks ready for the mayhem to begin. To this day I can still hear Bill shouting from the back, 'just be bloody careful Steve.....don't go back to a firework if it doesn't light properly', 'yes yes yes, daddy, don't worry' said Steve patronisingly. Needless to say, Steve, Neil and myself had decided that we'd start the display with umpteen fireworks going off simultaneously. Almost a finale in reverse! I don't recall precisely how many we lit each, but I suspect it was about 3. Given the small area where we were operating in, this had to be coordinated carefully. Needless to say, it wasn't! Having selected a few decent looking fireworks each, we randomly scattered them around the garden. On the word 'go' from Steve we'd each light our fireworks in quick succession and then decant to the patio area. But the operating area was small, the display experts a little inebriated and the lighting order and escape routes not discussed. '1,2,3...Go!' shouted Steve, followed by a rather pathetic frenzy as we scampered from firework to firework, 'where is it...I can't find the fuse' shouted Steve, 'mine are all lit...I'm off' shouted Neil, whilst I fumbled around in the dark trying to light my assigned fireworks, acutely aware that Neil's fuses were already going fast, time was running out!

However, by the grace of God Steve and myself managed *just* to get our fireworks lit in time and ran for our lives to the gathered crowd, who were laughing and jeering us on. 'come on lads, get on with it', 'should have got the professionals in Bill', 'bloody right, letting too many off at once there lads' came the voice of reason, 'can't send boys to do a man's job' came another shout to bouts of laughter. Then, in an instance the banter was over as all hell broke loose. The garden lit up in a blaze of colours but one of the fireworks had not been inserted into the ground firm enough and had fallen over. It fired its white-hot propellant slam into the garden fence, which then ricocheted over the gathered crowd, then slammed into the outhouse (where our secret booty was hidden) and then across the patio. It was pinball with fireworks! The party were running in all directions, with the majority trying to squeeze through the patio windows simultaneously. There were shrieks and shrills and the whole scene was like the opening scene in Die Hard as Armageddon broke loose. Bill's voice could be heard above the mayhem, 'I bloody told you to be careful. Dickheads'.

Then the garden was silent. The saga was over as soon as it's started. Steve was checking everyone over, 'is everyone

Ok. Is anyone hurt', in between bouts of laughter. It became apparent that everyone was fine and the party people crawled out of their bunkers one by one. The human nature loves a close scrape, that feeling of survival after a moment of sheer terror or exhilaration. It's why we go to theme parks to go on roller coasters, or sky diving for charity etc. Far from going mad the party were now shouting for joy, the alcohol clearly helped and there were bouts of laughter, pats on the back all round and much ribbing of Steve for nearly killing all his parent's family and friends. Of course, we'll never know who hadn't put their firework into the ground properly, but for the purpose of this book it was Steve…..trust me…..I'm also his best mate!

The rest of the firework display went without a hitch…..but not without several telling offs from Bill and a more controlled sequencing for letting them off. Soon enough we'd mullered our way through a small fortune of fireworks to the whoops and hollering from the party, 'there goes another £7.50…..hooray!!' Once the fireworks were expended, Val declared the buffet was now open, 'Ok everyone…. it's time to eat'.

The herd frantically made their way to the buffet starting point, where Steve's Nan Mary was already doing the honours of removing the protective coverings. The buffet was there in all its glory. Sausage rolls, chicken legs, beef and ham sandwiches, vol-au-vent's then sausage rolls, chicken legs, beef and ham sandwiches and vol-au-vent's and then the same again (so true Peter Kay), with lots of delicious sides and, right there in the centre of the table in all its glory as always was a rather majestic looking whole Salmon. I think every party I went to at Westmorland Avenue there was a whole

Salmon. It always looked fantastic, but alas I'm not one for the pink fish, so it passed me by every time. Having over faced themselves, the guests at a Redman party were always treated to a ridiculous array over calorific delights for desserts. Death by Chocolate being one of Steve's personal favourites. I was more of a savoury man and preferred an extra chicken leg or two rather than the desserts, but jolly good they always looked.

After the *good eat* the crowd were a little less raucous and folk dissipated into the kitchen and front living room. You know a party is easing off when the host starts asking if anyone would like a Gaelic Coffee. A taxi was called for Mary's ......Bill usually took care of that....and then the cries started (usually from me) for Bill to sing us a song. Bill usually remonstrated for an hour before relenting and his guitar was sprung from its hiding place. I shall discuss our sing-alongs in another chapter, suffice to say they were great fun and emotionally treasured moments. Eventually the guests started to bid farewell at an ever-increasing rate and the characteristic noise of taxis could be heard pulling up.

The remnants of the party now slouched on the sofas in the front room, Steve pulled me to one side and whispered, 'come on McAttack, time to let Big Bertha off', 'yeah ok Redders' and off we skulked to the outhouse. Our Scud Missile was still there, despite the freezer being invaded for additional ice cubes throughout the night, we hadn't been busted.

Steve cradled Big Bertha and we moved by torchlight to the back of the garden where the firework carcasses from the earlier display were strewn around the lawn. 'Right, there's a big tube that came with it over there, fetch it over' said Steve. Sure enough, in one of Val's flower beds was a drain pipe.

And I'm not kidding. It was bloody massive and not readily identifiable as a rocket launcher tube unless you were used to public firework displays.

Steve had brought with him a hammer, and after temporarily lying the rocket on the grass he hammered in the huge tube to a decent depth. 'Do you not think we're a little bit too near to the trees Steve, and plus the factory over the back has a glass roof'. I may have inadvertently forgotten to mention the factory over the fence at the back of Steve's parents' house. A major cause of concern for Bill when letting off the fireworks each year and earlier on in the evening when the 3 Amigos were doing their best to cause a catastrophe. 'Don't worry about it McAttack, it'll be well clear of the factory before it goes off…trust me'. Together we gingerly loaded the missile into the huge drainpipe, like 2 scientists carefully arming a nuclear bomb. Once in place we looked at each other with an air of concern, like we might get caught in the act, just like Guy Fawkes and his conspirators. 'Are you ready', Steve whispered. We were both nervous. The firework was ridiculously large, and a fear came over me as all of a sudden the garden seemed preposterously small……and maybe…. just maybe this was a bad idea?!

The firework lighting tappers were long gone, so Steve had brought some matches. 'Here goes' said Steve and he struck a match allowing it to take in the mild November evening. Westmorland Avenue lies very near to the seafront in Cleveleys and throughout the year is windswept. However, thankfully on the evening in question it was remarkably still. Just as well. Before we dwelt on things too long Steve lit the enormous fuse and we retreated swiftly to the patio doors at the back of the house.

The fuse seemed to take ages. And then there was an ALMIGHTY flash, so bright it lit up the whole of the house, neighbour's houses and adjacent factory! So intense was the sub-atomic explosion that I thought the thing had gone off on the ground. But I was wrong, this was merely the launch propulsion system and we were engulfed in cordite fumes as if we were standing on a launch pad at Cape Canaveral. Smoke billowed in through the patio doors, into the kitchen and on into the hallway. There was then an enormous THUMP…. like a land mortar being fired, for that it was it was, with a terrifying WOOOOSH that is hard to describe unless someone is stood only 20feet away from such a piece of kit. The firework accelerated so fast that our necks were strained as it reached for the heavens, screaming upwards to an orbital height, greater than that of Blackpool Tower. And then there was one CATACLYISMIC explosion so huge that it lit up the whole of Cleveleys. It was probably seen in both Fleetwood and Blackpool.

The burst was so unbelievably big that it shocked us, and we stood there like Beavis and Butthead, as jaws dropped, 'woawa' we said in unison. The firework was unbelievable and it had scared the living daylights out of us. We were in a state of utter shock. Then, rather abruptly, we were brought down to earth with a bump, 'STEVEN!!' shouted Bill as he was gaining nearer from the front living room, 'WHAT THE BLOODY HELL IS GOING ON, THE WHOLE STREET JUST LIT UP!!' shouted his dad in a rage of disbelief. 'There was one left in the box dad' Steve shouted back. As if that was going to wash!

Remember, remember the 5th of November for gunpowder treason and plot..........and 2 muppets from Blackpool can now also be added to the end of this immortalised nursery rhyme.

GREG MCEVOY

Cadet McEvoy

Cadet Redman

Summer Camp 1986, RAF Church Fenton
Prior to Steve's arrival at ATC 2501 Squadron

Fun in the Sun

Good Times

TRUST ME...I'M YOUR BEST MATE!

Steve's Wedding Day 2001    Greg's Wedding Day 2002

Steve's Wedding Day – Overlooking the River Glomma

Where's that Glider?    No Explanation..

CHAPTER 9 – TRUST ME…
I'M YOUR BEST MATE
Whitesnake – Bad Boys

The following story is infamous within our respective family circles. It featured during Steve's wedding to Ellen in 2001, where I was his Best Man, much to the delight of the guests, who were predominantly Norwegian. It is indeed the title of this book and was probably top of our *riskier* exploits. None of the following is invented………you couldn't make it up……

It was a pretty non-descript winters evening, a Thursday if I recall correctly, and it was that strange period on the Fylde Coast where the holiday season has ended, following the switch off of the Blackpool illuminations at the end of October, but before the *mad* festive season starts. This is when the swathes of office parties get underway at the many hotels, bars and restaurants throughout the resort. The rest of the year Blackpool was alive with tourists and a great place to live. Looking back we were spoilt for choice with Theatres, Piers, The famous Blackpool Tower with its truly stunning ball room, ice rink, cinemas, indoor water park, bowling alleys, crown green bowling, golf courses (including Royal Lytham of The Open fame), crazy golf, casinos, Trams, the thrill of the Pleasure Beach, umpteen top end Night Clubs, bars and restaurants galore, the golden mile, the illuminations and of course 7 miles of sandy beach. As I said in an earlier chapter, what folk did in other towns across the UK I do not know, all I know was that Blackpool was a hive of activity, fun and alive!

On this particular evening, at least for Steve and myself, there was 'nowt much happening'! We were in our late teens and of an age that were easily bored sat indoors. It certainly wasn't the thing to do to be sat in with the oldies! I think I was about 19 and Steve 18. Either way, I recall we were legally entitled to enter licenced premises so, despite it being a rather bleak and boring mid-week evening, it was pretty odds on that we'd be out somewhere. This was the early 1990's and mobile phones had yet to really take off with the general populous. They might have been common place in Canary Warf at the time with the City yuppies, but they were bloody expensive, unreliable and the size and weight of a brick.

Steve and myself were still firmly living in a world where if you wanted someone you either used the landline, and risked enquiring conversations with your mate's parents, or you popped over to see them.

It was always an excuse to get out of the house and go for a drive too, so I always preferred the latter. So, on this dismal nothing of an evening I sauntered the 5 miles along the promenade to Cleveleys to catch up with Steve but with no plan. I had only been driving a couple of years and still had my first car, a Vauxhall Chevette. Some reading this will have no idea what a Vauxhall Chevette looks like? May I suggest at this point you put down this book and Google or Bing it on your smart phone. I can guarantee that you'll be suitably underwhelmed. However, at the time it was reliable, pretty nifty and my means of getting from A to B. But I'm not going to say I was in love with it!

It was dark as I drove down the promenade under the canopy of street lighting from Gynn Square up to Bispham, past the enormous Norbreck Castle Hotel then through the centre of Cleveleys where the Tramlines turn inland a mile from the seafront towards Fleetwood. I arrived at Steve's house, which was located at the north end of Cleveleys, not far from Rossall. Whilst I'd known Steve a good few years by this point, I never let myself in. I always knocked and waited for his mum or dad to answer the front door. I was always made to feel welcome and greeted in like a returning prodigal son. Having exchanged pleasantries with his mum I ventured up the narrow staircase on the right-hand side of the hall to Steve's bedroom. The framed Lamborghini photos and Sam & Fox Goldfish now long gone. 'Hey up McAttack, how we doing' greeted Steve. 'Not sure, nothing going on really, fancy the Sandpiper' came my reply. The Sandpiper was the local Pub across the road. It was a good Pub, and had a community feel about it. But it was, at the end of the day, a modern 'Nags Head' as of Only Fools & Horses fame i.e. a Local Pub in the true sense of the word and I just sensed that Steve would be looking for a little more adventure. 'Nah…..no chance, let's get out somewhere. Someone told me they've a Karaoke on at Mr Dales tonight, let's give that a try'. Cue furrowed brow on my part, 'Mr Dales! It's a grab a Granny dive pal. No chance! And I am not doing Karaoke that's for sure!', came my retort. I should make clear at this point that Karaoke was a pretty new phenomenon, a craze sweeping the nation, very much a Japanese import, possibly made famous by the Australian broadcaster Clive James in his various observational TV shows on the weird and wonderful.

But Steve had one over me. 'Right McAttack, there's nothing going on in Blackpool and I don't fancy going up these anyway. So, let's go and have a look and if we don't like it the KFC is on me. How about that? And anyway……have you ever done Karaoke?'. Damn, he had me! 'err no……but it's not for me.

I can't sing and I am not making myself look like a fool. Besides, somebody I know might see me!'. "Someone you know might see you! Are you having a laugh? Who do you know that goes in Mr Dales'? came Steve's reply. 'OK' said Steve, still laughing to himself, 'I'll do the singing and drinking, you can do the driving'. 'Fair enough' I ventured and with that Steve grabbed his jacket and we were off. Given that the Karaoke didn't get started properly until 9pm Steve suggested that we hit the Beach Tavern in Cleveleys first for a couple of cheeky pints, or in my case a couple of Britvic 55's......I was never a fan of Cola. The Beach Tavern was located not far from Cleveleys main high-street and stood on the corner on Beach Road.....funnily enough only a very short distance from the beach. It was well known in the area for live acts. Steve and myself frequented the pub quite regularly to watch local rock bands, Stiff Richard at the time being our favourite. However, there were rows of empty seats on this bleak winter's night which said it all. We passed the time quietly enough at the Beach Tavern in the lack lustre atmosphere munching crisps and catching up. But 30 minutes was enough, so we jumped back in the Chevette and headed towards Mr Dales.

Mr Dales was only a mile or so away and lay between Cleveleys and Bispham (both north of Blackpool) in the Little Bispham area. It sat at the end of an incredibly potholed private road and bizarrely located next to a golf driving range and Par3 9-hole golf course. All the buildings and facilities survive 37 years on....and the road is still as potholed as it was back then! Nothing has changed. Either way, Mr Dales was Cleveleys & Bispham's *only nightclub*. It was a last resort if you were looking to stay out late (sorry but it was true). Don't forget, this was in an era when Pubs shouted for last orders at 10:50 and called time at 11:00. Nightclubs were allowed to stay open later but the same rule applied, last orders at 01:50 and time called at 02:00. In both instances you were allowed 20minutes or so to finish your drink, but if you hadn't it was tough luck and you were literally thrown out! Nowadays the younger folk start their evenings when I'm going to bed and party hard until 06:00! Not for me, I enjoy my mornings too much.

On arriving we parked up in the large and fairly empty carpark and made our way in. There were no windows at Mr Dales, well…. there were but they were boarded up and painted black. Inside the Club was compact but had enough space for maybe 200-300 punters. It was all black inside and burgundy seating with a rather dodgy air about it. However, on the evening in question I recall being pleasantly surprised that there were people in and who seemed to be having a good time. I also have a recollection of it being cold in there though, as if the proprietor had deliberately left the heating off, banking on a good crowd to generate sufficient body heat. The Karaoke was indeed in full swing and I guess there were 20 - 30 people around the dance floor area. I scanned the faces but didn't recognise anyone. Phew! We sat down in a corner and noted immediately that there were menus on the table. Karaoke menus that is! We hadn't even bought a drink and Steve was scanning the menu like a deranged idiot, clearly looking for his 2 favourites 'Achy Breaky Heart' or 'Three Steps to Heaven', but as it happened my luck was in and this was a decent Karaoke menu so he couldn't find them! Or was my luck in? 'Right Mr McEvoy, what we singing', 'hang on…. back right-up Redder's, I never said I was singing, in fact the deal was that you would and I wouldn't'! 'You're right, but I tell you Greg, you've got to try everything once in your life to decide if you like it or not, that's my motto', 'well it's bloody well not my motto……not doing it, and besides, someone I know might see me!'. Steve was up for dealing with my protests, 'Look. Why don't we sing one together? I'll pick something we know, maybe Bon Jovi….and I'll buy the beers……..a bit of Dutch courage, you can have a couple right'? Hmmm…..he was testing me here. 'Come on, there's nobody in here that we know'…..I mused over this momentarily, 'go on then but ONLY if we do something together….and you're buying the beer…..and make sure you ask the DJ to call us up later on……I'm not doing it right now'! Steve chuckled, 'OK. You're such a wimp but go on then. I'll go and talk to the DJ to see what he has in terms of easy rock numbers that we know then I'll get the beers', and off he went leaving me suitably spooked that I'd agreed to this.

A few minutes later Steve arrived with 2 cold pints of beer and sat down, 'right sorted, he'll call us up in 30-40 minutes. Steve gestured to the lively bunch of ladies sat behind us, 'this lot have put a load of requests in ahead of us. Sure enough there was a group of ladies in their 30's sat a few yards away enjoying themselves.

So, we sat there watching the night draw out as a range of amateur singers paraded onto the stage to knock out a song you could barely recognise. As time marched on my confidence grew owing to i) the limited talent on display this evening, ii) the relaxed atmosphere and iii) the Dutch courage. On the subject of Dutch courage, Steve suggested another one might help with the nerves and so he sauntered off to buy himself another pint.

Whilst I would have liked another and it wasn't strong beer, we acknowledged that 1 was enough given I was driving.

'OK ladies and gents......next up it's Steve and Greg who are going to do a duet and a rock number too.....come on boys let's have you up here' exclaimed the DJ as the whooping started from the group of ladies watching on who were now *well on their way*. The nerves really kicked in now for me. It was alright for Steve, he was used to this malarkey and, judging from what I was about to hear, he was and still is clearly deluded about his vocal capabilities. But it really wasn't for me. I *knew* I couldn't sing, so why try!

We crossed the small wooden dancefloor and climbed a couple of steps up onto the stage. As we did so I asked Steve what track he had asked for, thinking how remiss I'd been for not asking beforehand? 'Whitesnake' came his reply. We were both rock fiend's and very much into that genre, which was very popular during the 1980's and early 1990's. Whitesnake were right up there for Steve and myself and still are some 37-years on. 'OK, nice one Steve' came my reply. The DJ, one of those self-indulged witty individuals who like to deride folk at any opportunity, passed us a microphone each, 'looking forward to this one lad's' he said in a rather sarcastic manner. *Cheeky sod* I thought, as we strategically placed ourselves in front of the large TV monitor where we would be able to read the lyrics. The whoops and hollering started now from the well lubricated audience of approximately 30 people, in particular the group of ladies who were now becoming a little raucous. The Hooch alco-pops were definitely taking effect with them! But Steve and myself were ready to go, microphones in hand.

And then the night unravelled in an instance. Steve's dad, god bless him, would have referred to this going pear-shaped *big-time*! I knew every Whitesnake song written over the preceding decade inside out and back to front. I owned a complete album collection and listened to them frequently.... I still do. They are my favourite rock band of all time. I had been waiting with high expectation for a heavy metal guitar rift to kick in loud and fast. But as soon as I heard the opening notes, I knew instantly something was massively wrong!!! Instead of a heavy metal guitar, a soft and haunting synthesizer sound kicked in and gentle guitar rhythm. I looked at Steve in utter panic, but internally knowing the answer, 'what did you pick?' I said with anguish written across my face and now completely thrown as to what was happening.

Steve looked at me without so much as a care in the world, 'Is This Love'. Sweet Jesus mother of Mary! This was my WORST nightmare! Here we were, two local idiots on the stage at Mr Dales singing a bloody rock love ballad! *Is This Love* is without question a true rock ballad classic, but it wasn't something I wanted to be doing in a duet with my best mate on a karaoke night!!! I just couldn't believe it, what an absolute moron, I was incredulous! Why, oh why oh why....it beggared belief! Redman had struck again *big time*. Even worse, I knew that three quarters of the way through that track David Coverdale hits an incredibly high note, some 2 or 3 octaves higher........we didn't stand a chance! But there we were, fully committed, no chance of running, trapped on Mr Dales' stage. The group of ladies now on their feet arms aloft swaying side to side and the odd cigarette lighter flame flickering in the air. What a complete and utter disaster!!!

It felt to me like we were on a runaway train and had no choice but to crack on with the song. I gave Steve umpteen looks that would kill, which he seemed to find funny. However, things were about to deteriorate even further! Whilst well into the 2nd verse, as if it couldn't possibly get any worse, the double-doors leading from the nightclub entrance flung open and in came a crowd of around 10 people.

Instantly I recognised ALL of them!! The colour drained from my face. At the time I was working in the Civil Service and a gentleman at the far end of my office was retiring. I didn't really know him so well, having not worked there that long, so hadn't gone out on the leaving celebrations. But I was aware of the planned night out and recognised most of the faces that had now entered the Club.

It was apparent that they'd all been *on the booze,* since early doors as they were incredibly giddy and practically holding one another up. This motley crew were clearly the remnants of the party...... and they were completely bladdered. The abuse started instantly. 'whey hey.....look it's McEvoy' shouted one of them, 'come on lads.....is this love that I'm feeling' came the chorus from a few of them. They were besides themselves in drunken hysterics. I was fuming, completely embarrassed and wanted the ground to open up and swallow me. We brought the house down with laughter when we realised that our tight jeans weren't tight enough and we crashed and burned on the high note near the end of the track. This was by far the biggest disaster Steve had ever gotten me into! The song finished and I dumped my microphone into the extended hand of the DJ, 'alright chump, well done lads' came his reply whilst laughing to himself.

I can't tell you how fast I was off that stage and across the dance floor to our seats. Total embarrassment. The DJ was still besides himself and some derogatory comment was made as we scuppered away back to our seats. The drunken crowd made their way to the bar for more alcohol that they clearly didn't need. No doubt the next morning they wouldn't have a clue. But 37 years on I recall vividly that embarrassing encounter! Little did I know at that point that the night was to get even worse.......

We finished our drinks in short order and made our way for the exit, 'come on McAttack let's get something to eat' said Steve. Not even the lure of a KFC on this evening was going to recover this disaster, 'I'm not bothered pal, I think I'm just going to get off but I'll drop you off first'. 'Fair enough', came the reply and thus we jumped into my blue Chevette for the short drive to Steve's house. The roads were deadly quiet, it was as if the world had turned in for the night. To get to Steve's house we had to drive through Cleveleys centre once more and cross Victoria Road West. There were other routes to his house but this was the most direct. During the weekend Victoria Road West, the high street that runs through the centre of Cleveleys, is a very busy shopping street and a popular destination for tourists from Blackpool who can catch a Tram from the big and brash seaside resort down to Cleveleys Town Centre, which had a more sedate and relaxing feel about it. However, as I slowed to a halt at the red traffic lights, Victoria Road West was deserted. Not even a car. Looking back, I suspect it was probably around 11pm. There wasn't a soul to be seen. We sat in silence waiting for the lights to change, only the quiet drum of the car engine ticking over.

I recall sat there looking ahead at the greyness of the Royal Bank of Scotland building on the corner, and at how austere it looked. It almost said as much about the night. We waited and waited..... and waited. Nothing. No amber light. We waited a little longer. Still nothing. I leaned across the dashboard to see the lights on the other side but it was clear nothing was happening. Still looking ahead at the lights, I commented to Steve, 'I think the lights are jammed'. Still nothing and we were both growing impatient, 'I think you're right', replied Steve. We gave it a further 20 seconds or so, still nothing and no traffic around or persons to be seen. 'Sod it, let's go' and with that I accelerated away looking left and right but nothing to be seen. 'Holy crap!' shouted Steve 'Cops! You've jumped a light step on it!!!'

Sure enough, tucked down an adjacent alley way was a Police Van and as I'd accelerated across the road it was as if they'd been lying in wait and pounced. 'Accelerate, turn right here' shouted Steve as we zipped down a side street. 'Turn right again' and we crossed the Tram tracks and shot down another residential side street.

I genuinely don't recall seeing the Police Van in pursuit and wasn't even sure I'd done anything wrong given the electrical failure of the traffic light system, but Steve was adamant we should clear the area pronto! 'Take another right here' shouted Steve taking us this time down an alley. 'Right, dump the car here' he said whilst looking over his shoulder, 'I'm not leaving my car here?' I said in a quizzical yet frenzied manner. 'You've just jumped a light' leave it here and we can get it later or tomorrow'. So, we got out of the car and ran off down the alley. This all felt rather surreal and my head was spinning as to why we were having to do this.....but Steve was adamant and turned to me, 'trust me....I'm your best mate'! Who was I to argue? For the next 20 minutes we acted like 2nd World

War downed Airmen leaping from garden to garden with the German Army (Police) in hot pursuit……even if I hadn't seen them. Had Steve imagined all this? Would we have been in trouble given the circumstances?
Despite youth being on our side eventually we tired and one last wall scaled found us in a Church Graveyard panting for breath. 'Bloody hell Redman, you don't half get us in some scrapes', 'don't blame me, you jumped the light and you had a beer at Mr Dales….they'll throw the key away if they get hold of you. Let's stay here for a while.

You can stop at mine tonight and get the car in the morning. Trust me on this one'. After about 15- or 20-minutes waiting, and now fully recovered, Steve advised on our next move. 'Right, you stay there behind the big headstone there' as he pointed to quite a large grey memorial to someone long departed. 'I ain't stopping in a graveyard on my own you dilbert!' I exclaimed. 'You scared you big wuss', came Steve's ever sympathetic tone, 'they're all dead in here you know….they ain't gonna get you'. He paused momentarily, 'look. Just sit tight and I'll go and see if the coast is clear' and with that he was off like a stealthy SAS operative.

I sat waiting. My overwhelming view was that this had been all completely unnecessary and over the top and that we should have explained that the lights weren't working to the Police….but then maybe my best mate was right after all?

It was starting to get cold and, whilst Steve had probably only been gone for 10 or 15 minutes it felt like an eternity. My night vision had taken hold and the graveyard didn't appear quite as dark as it had when I'd arrived. I also didn't feel any concern about sharing this hallowed ground with our long-departed brethren. I was more concerned about the time that was elapsing and the concern that my parents might have given I said that I wouldn't be home late. As mentioned already, this was in the days before mobile phones became common place.

After what felt like about 30 minutes, but which was probably less, I was growing concerned for Steve. I decided to go and have a look myself to see if the coast was clear and, before pondering too long, in an instance I climbed over the wall and headed towards the alley where I'd left my car. I walked normally down the Street at a reasonable pace, scanning all around for sight of Steve and /or the Police....but nothing. I reached the alley way and stopped next to a building drainpipe. I then gingerly peeked my forehead round the corner. To my absolute horror there were 2 Policemen looking over my car. I wasn't parked illegally but they were looking it over. That was it. Decision made. I'm out of here and I turned to return to the graveyard as fast as I could!

I scaled the wall and landed fairly hard on the other side scaring the life out of Steve who'd retuned unbeknown to me, 'holy crap McAttack!' as I landed in the grass verge, 'I thought you were a bleeding ghost! Where have you been! I thought you'd been nicked!'. Catching my breath I replied, 'I went to look for you. I thought you'd gone home. There are Police looking over the car'. Steve glared at me, 'I know you plonker! That's why I told you to stay here! Come on. You can stop at mine'. And with that we headed off in the opposite direction towards Steve's house, compelled to leave my car until the morning. However, I was still unsure that I'd done much wrong and could have explained things to the Police...

After 15minutes or so we reached Steve's house which was cloaked in darkness. Steve gingerly put his key in the front door and pushed it forward. As we entered the hallway he whispered, 'just sleep in the back room on the couch there. I'll get you a blanket. We can get the car in the morning'. However, before we got any further there was the thud, thud, thud as someone walked across the bedroom above and the landing light went on, 'Steve. Is that you!' came a very stern call from Bill, Steve's father, 'errm…..yes Dad, that's me home', 'is Greg with you?!'….'err…yes he is as it happens'.

Then came a very angry, gruff retort never to be forgotten in the remaining years that Bill was with us, 'well what the bloody hell have you two been up to, I've had the bloody Lancashire Constabulary on the phone and Greg's parents! WHAT THE HELL HAVE YOU BEEN UP TO?!' came the blast as he came charging down the stairs. 'You need to get on the phone to your parents rapid Greg and then the Police'. Eeek. This was NOT good. Bill had a great deal of time for me, but on this occasion, he was fuming. 'You' he said pointing to Steve. 'get to your room'. 'You' he said pointing to myself, 'You need to get on to your parents ASAP and your mum will come and get you'. Bill was a fantastic bloke and became a true friend and companion in the years to come. But this was the maddest I'd ever seen him and it was to be the angriest I'd ever see him.

I gingerly picked up the telephone handset and dialled home. My Dad answered and the chastising started again, 'What the bloody hell have you and Steve been up to?! We've had the Police on 3 times looking to speak to you! They want to know if your car has been stolen! Where are you now?'. This wasn't great, in fact this was as bad as it got and would ever get. 'I'm at Steve's house', 'right, stay there. Do not move. You're Mum's coming to get you now'. And with that the line went dead.

I turned to Bill, Steve's now gone to his room, tail firmly between his legs. I looked at Bill with remorseful eyes, 'my mum is coming to pick me up, she'll be here in 10 minutes'. Bill glared at me, 'I don't know what you've been up to but I don't want nothing to do with it', and with that he resided to the kitchen where he lit up a cigarette, not prepared to enter conversation, just to wait patiently until I'd been collected to be *dealt with*. Within what felt like a very short space of time my mother pulled up outside in the family silver Rover. A comfortable executive car, but poorly built and full of the usual British Leyland idiosyncrasies. I didn't say goodbye to Bill, but he glanced at me from the kitchen as I slipped out of the front door quietly.

Then I got it again, 'what the bloody hell have you been up to!? Your Dad is going mad? Where is your car? Get in!'. A full volley of salvos but deliberately not given the opportunity to answer in between the passing shots.....not that I felt like answering. I was, by now, feeling rather sorry for myself. I got into the car and sat sheepishly as my mum pulled away. Nothing was said but she was clearly fuming...albeit quietly. The journey home was about 5 miles. We didn't drive back through the centre of Cleveleys, perhaps just as well, but instead took a back route towards Anchorsholme.

We did however pass Mr Dales Nightclub as we headed towards Bispham.....had I really been singing *Is This Love* in there only a few hours ago? It all felt surreal. However, the nights drama still wasn't over! As we neared the halfway point between Cleveleys and Bispham, not far from the Red Lion Pub, a blue flashing light became apparent behind us and rapidly drew nearer. Eventually the Police car started to flash furiously indicating for my mum to pull over. My heart sank, I was done for, but there was also a feeling of relief that the evenings antics would be dealt with and I could try to explain myself……not that I was expecting to be believed! I looked at my mum, the game was up and, with tears in my eyes muttered, 'sorry mum…..it's me they are after'. My mum looked at me and in a surprisingly soft voice said, 'what on earth have you done'. Soon enough a Police officer walked up and tapped on the window. It was game set and match……..or was it? 'Good evening madam. Do you realise that this is a 30mph zone'? Well knock me down with a feather duster! It wasn't me they were after……it was my mum….for speeding!! Fortunately, my mother was only marginally over the 30mph limit and, following a warning on adhering to the speed limits we were allowed on our way. What a turn of events!

We sat in silence for the rest of the journey, the irony was palpable. We drove on through Bispham, up past the North Shore Golf Club on our right-hand side and finally past the large monolithic looking Water Tower in North Shore Blackpool, that could be seen for miles around, before taking a right turn onto Warbreck Hill Road where we lived. Soon enough we were home. I guess it was late, maybe 12:30am.

My dad was waiting in the living room for my 3rd and final dressing down of the evening – it crossed my mind that Steve was probably fast asleep by now, dreaming of our next escapade. As I entered the living room my dad was stood up next to the large Victorian Fireplace. 'What the bloody hell have you been up to!!' came the blast and a look that could kill, eyes bulging. Looking back my response was rather shameful, 'don't have a go at me! I think you'll find it's mum who has been cautioned by the Police for speeding!'. My Dad looked dumfounded and sideways at my Mum. I think I qualified the situation, 'well....it was a warning on this occasion'. My Dad looked at me, ignoring what I had just said, 'where's your car?', 'I left it in Cleveleys'. I think my Dad knew the script, 'had you been drinking?', 'I only had 1 but the traffic lights wouldn't work. We drove through them as they weren't working'! I got one last almighty blast, 'get to your bed!'. I'd had enough fun for 1 day and beat a hasty retreat. I didn't sleep well.

The car was recovered the next morning but not before I had to report to Cleveleys Police Station to retrieve the HT leads, which had been removed for security given the car was unlocked. I had a rather frank exchange with the Officer just coming off night duty, but I'll keep that conversation to myself. Once back at the vehicle I also had the pleasure of removing a complaint left on my windscreen for blocking someone's garage (for which I was truly sorry). I started the engine and sat there momentarily reflecting on the night before, *trust me, I'm your best* mate ran through my mind and I let out a wry smile. A mantra to be heard for years to come. For sure, neither Steve or myself wanted another night like that in a hurry! I drove off home thinking of the apology I owed Steve's parents and which I would address that evening........never a dull moment indeed.....

CHAPTER 10 - MALE MODELS
The Prodigy – Firestarter

Not all the escapades recorded in this book are long tales. Indeed, this next short but sweet adventure has a gem of an ending and it still haunts me to this day!

During the mid-1990's Steve found himself working as a DJ on the Mediterranean Cruise liners and, after 3 years of fun in the sun, ended up DJ'ing Nightclubs and Bars in Norway. Indeed, how this ex-RAF Airman had gotten himself into this line of business is another story in itself. The abridged version of events is that on one fine summer evening I sat down at the dining table to pen a best man's speech, given Steve's wedding day was looming nearer. This was his 2nd engagement, so there was a degree of confidence this time round! I had barely started to write my speech when the house phone started ringing. My Dad answered it and shouted me through to the hallway advising that Steve's Dad Bill was on the line for me. I knew this was going to be interesting as his Dad NEVER rang my Mum and Dad's house. A rather short conversation followed, 'have you started writing that Best Man's speech yet Greg?', 'err, no Bill why?', 'because he's gone', 'erm..ok…gone where?' I replied. 'He's buggered off on the cruise liners DJ'ing, the wedding's off, he's already out of the country. Thought I'd save you the time and effort with that speech. Anyway, take care and I'll let you know when we hear from him'. 'Err….ok, Bill. Thanks'. And that was it. Steve had left the UK and wasn't to return to the home shores for many years, apart from trips home to visit family and friends. But his time overseas certainly led to many excellent adventures together!

Fast forward a few years to the mid 1990's and Steve was working in central Norway, in the town of Kongsberg. He had a contract working at a hotel with its own nightclub, which only required him to work a couple of nights per week. Having free live in accommodation he'd invited me over to stay, to have a few beers and a catch up. Even better he'd talked a fellow DJ into covering his slots at the Club, so we had a long weekend to party hard!

The journey to Norway was uneventful and I flew to Torp Sandesjord Airport, approx. 1.5hrs south of Oslo, but that has a shuttle bus service to the City Centre that I had no trouble getting. Steve kindly arranged for one of his English pals, a translator who lived in Oslo, to meet me at the Bus Station and ensure that I safely got on the right bus to Kongsberg. I'm sure I would have been fine, but it was a nice gesture nonetheless. Having gotten on the bus all I had to do was sit back and enjoy the journey. I don't recollect too much as it was the depths of winter so dark after not too long and before I knew it I'd fallen asleep.

After maybe an hour or so I came to, which was just as well as the bus was on the outskirts of Kongsberg. It was late in the evening now and exceptionally cold, circa -12 degrees, with deep snow all around. As the bus came to a halt and the passengers disembarked, I strained to look forward to see if Steve was there? Whilst I couldn't see him at first as I clambered down from the bus true to form Steve was there ready and waiting….and full of beans! 'How ya doing McAttack?! Long day? Ooo, I'm sure we can squeeze a few Sherberts in! You hungry?'. I think it is impossible for Steve to get through any social encounter without uttering these words, words I have heard for the last 35 years....... *are you hungry?* A cue to Steve spending a significant amount of cash on copious amounts of food. Why choose something to eat, when you can choose everything to eat. No?

After finding an establishment that was still open and filling our faces with a huge American beef burger with all the trimmings, a couple of bottles of beer and caught up on what he'd been up to, we headed off back to the hotel. It was a large multi-storey hotel and painted white. It was located right in the centre of the town, so ideal for getting out and about and not far at all from either the Bus or Rail stations. After a guided tour of the Hotel and a quick look at the Nightclub where he worked (which was already starting to fill with punters) we headed off for a good night's sleep.

The next morning, I felt fresh as a daisy and ready to go.... although as per usual, Steve's nocturnal behaviour and inability to make use of any time before 11am, mean that I spent the morning waiting for the slumbering giant to stir. It must be said, this is like waiting for an Orchid to bloom. One has to be patient. There can be many false alarms. But I have found that placing a Mars Bar and a full fat can of coke next to his bedside - and directly within his line of sight - can reduce the waiting time...albeit marginally. It's the flickering eye lids...if they just capture the coke can.....then there's a chance of ending the coma like state.

After waiting a small eternity, the beast from the east managed to lift his head, 'urrgh...morning'....and then he was straight into the calorific breakfast. After waiting an eternity and several attempts at going back to sleep, he finally grabbed a shower and started to make a serious attempt at entering the land of the living.

At last, we were ready to go! 'Right, you hungry? Let's go and get some lunch'. So, off we went to find a small café in the high street. Over lunch Steve announced the plans for the rest of the day, which was a beautiful gin-clear but exceptionally cold Saturday. 'First of all, we're heading off to an indoor sports complex', this was a revelation, Steve doesn't do sports, he continued, 'they have ice-hockey, indoor electronic golf, arcade machines and indoor bowling'. Superb I thought, some thought gone into this!. 'Then, McAttack, I have lined us up with a special treat' Hmmm. Things were going too smoothly on this trip and I'd clocked the glint in his eye', 'what special treat?'.........'well, when I was in Oslo last month DJ'ing, I met two absolutely stunning girls. Unbelievably attractive. I've told them you're coming over, so they're catching the train over from Oslo tonight. One each I thought for a date night, we're meeting them at 7pm at the station'. I wasn't amused. Here we go again. Another Redman disaster looming. 'You've done what?! Why do you do these things!'. 'Well thanks mate' said Steve, 'I line us up with two models and you have a paddy. You should be thanking me, not cursing me! Jeez, the thanks I get!'. 'Hang on, you've lined us up with 2 models!', 'yep sure have McAttack. Good eh!'. At this stage I had my head in my hands, 'so, you're telling me that 2 girls that are Norwegian Models are getting the train over here to meet us? Why on earth would they do that.... they haven't even met me'!

And then there was the look on Steve's face that butter wouldn't melt, a look I had seen a thousand times before. I smelt a rat. 'Go on. What's the catch Redman?'. 'Errm.... well....it was only a little lie that I told them', 'tell me now! What have you told them?!'. Steve, looking like the scalded child, eventually spilt the beans, 'errm.....I told them that you

were a male model and did gigs in London, New York and Paris......but don't shout at me, cos at least they're coming over!. I wanted to kill him, 'YOU'VE TOLD THEM WHAT?! THAT I'M A BLOODY SUPER MODEL!!. Christ Almighty! You've really landed us in it this time Redman'!! Steve was clearly amused by this outburst, 'Relax, everything will be fine. Our good humour will carry us far. Besides, I never said you were a *super model*, just a model'. As per usual, the clown was chuckling away. OMG, here we go again I thought to myself.
Yet another fine mess he'd gotten us into. I could barely relax and enjoy the afternoon thinking about the impending meeting.

The rest of the afternoon we spent enjoying ourselves at the complex and a few beers were had. But I kept thinking about the evening to come and the huge disappointment these 2 girls were in for. I am a natural worrier.....it's in my DNA.....and I was feeling uncomfortable about the whole situation, but I tried to put it to the back of my mind.

Soon enough the afternoon was spent and it was time to head back to the hotel to freshen up and grab something to eat before our 'evening date'. In Norway at this time of year not only is it perishing cold, but the daylight hours are incredibly short and even before getting back to the hotel it was already dark. The vivid colour that the winter sun had so briefly illuminated the town with had quickly diminished leaving a rather grey and dismal feel about the place. Back at the hotel I knew Steve was 'on a mission' as the pace continued. Usually he'd have 'hit the sack' for an hour or so, no question.

However, tonight it was straight into the shower, a splash of High Karate after shave and donned his best togs. With some more money now in his pocket Steve was ready and raring to go. This was unheard of, Steve being ready before me! But then, I was dragging my feet.

Soon enough we were both ready to go. Thick winter coats on and we were ready to rumble. I recall we visited the hotel bar for some Dutch courage, all costing a small fortune given sky-high Norwegian prices. 'Relax McAttack.......everything is going to be fine. Just chill, have a few drinky poos.......it will be fun'. I think he could tell on my face I wasn't convinced. Now, some reading this will be thinking, *what on earth is his problem, get on with it man*?! True. Any normal single bloke might take it all in his stride. However, you need to be aware that even at this point in my life I'd know Steve for at least 15years. Nothing is done by halves or with a sense of normality. Something untoward lurks round every corner and I was firmly of the opinion these girls were in for some disappointment.

Off we went by foot towards Kongsberg Rail Station. A small station that led right into the heart of this sleepy Norwegian Town. The walk was only a few minutes and there we were stood on an open dimly lit platform, nobody else there but us and our breath hanging in the sub-zero temperature. It struck me that this might not happen? I began to convince myself that Steve had held a conversation with these ladies a few weeks earlier in a busy and noisy nightclub whilst DJ'ing and, for sure, they wouldn't be turning up.

My mind wandered.......even if they did turn up, surely, they wouldn't remember or care for the fact that Steve's UK Male Model friend was coming over for the weekend? Surely that wasn't a selling point for them to spend time and money travelling on a train up from Oslo? No, that would be quite shallow. I looked over at Steve who was growing impatient, 'they ain't coming are they Steve' I asked as we kicked our heels (and the snow!) on the platform. All of a sudden Steve's expression changed, 'well we'll find out soon enough McAttack......here comes the train'! And he was right......we were fully committed now....the train was pulling into the station.

The train grew larger and was soon upon us grinding to a halt. A huge beast of a diesel with snowplough on the front, its work for the night over.

Some doors began to open and a very small number of passengers got off. Steve was busy scanning to identify our dates for the evening.....but he seemed to be struggling to spot them. Maybe, just maybe it was all about to unravel?

And then Steve proclaimed 'ah ha......they're here.....look!'. And sure enough, walking down the platform were two absolutely stunning Norwegian girls, one brunette and one blonde. 'Oh, my God Steve' I muttered under my breath but loud enough for Steve to hear. 'I know....good eh!'. Once again, he'd completely misunderstood, 'Good? No! Punching way, way, way above our heads here pal! Why oh why oh why...'. 'Shut up stumpy and relax....they're nearly here' came the reply. It then struck me that Steve hadn't even told me their names! 'Steve, I don't know their names', 'don't worry, I'll introduce you'. And then they were with us, two beautiful Scandinavian Models, a bit younger than I had thought they would be but very smiley and giggly and clearly very attractive. 'Hi Steve, great to see you, you're looking good'.....etc etc....plenty of cheek kissing ensued between the 3 of them, as is common place in continental Europe.......whilst I stood there watching.......always the gooseberry.

Finally, after the 3 had reacquainted themselves with one another and paid a sufficient number of compliments that seemed to go on for ages. Steve turned to introduce me. What followed next might be described as priceless. I'm not sure to this day whether Steve had really thought through what he was going to say, or whether he was once again setting me up for one almighty fall. I cannot recall the names of the beautiful ladies in question, but for ease we will call them Ingrid and Eva. For sure, I had not planned or contemplated what was about to happen next......

'Ingrid, Eva....please let me introduce you to Greg. He's my friend from London. The model I told you all about'. Holy Moses, I wanted the ground to open up and swallow me! It wasn't enough to lie to get them here but it was the first thing he wanted to impress them with! It was about to get worse... 'Hi Greg, great to meet you'.......more cheek kissing, this time for me......then came Steve's bomb shell for which I shall never forgive him, not even 20 years later....'yes, been a male model for a while has Greg.......quite busy at the moment....loads of assignments......wasn't it New York you were working in last week'? I wanted to punch him. I had never heard such a blatant lie said with more conviction in my life and now even worse I had 3 pairs of eyes looking at me eagerly for a response.

If looks could kill then Steve caught one right between the eyes, my response through gritted teeth, 'yes that's right, New York.....bit of a one off really'. And then just when I thought it couldn't get any worse it did. Ingrid, the beautiful blonde smiling away hit me with a question, 'wow...that's great Greg...New York, you are so lucky. Must be a big fashion house you were working for no? We're models too. What lines do you model'? I stumbled; my brain confused, a thousand thoughts, racing through my mind, desperately scrambling for a suitable answer. I felt cornered as all stood in silence waiting for my response. This good Catholic boy, trained not to tell lies, thrust into this scenario of deceit and a date with someone who should have been meeting Patrick Swayze….not Greg from Blackpool. My response shall go down in history. 'Oh….erm…I model gloves'. Steve's jaw dropped and the two Norwegian stunners looked confused, 'gloves?', came the reply, 'err….yes, gloves like these ones on my hands'. This is the most surreal experience in my life. Stood on a dimly lit platform in sub-zero temperatures, in a grey and cold Norwegian Town, with my best pal and two beautiful ladies and myself…….the glove model from London! Ha ha! That will teach Steve to set me up!

In an instance I'd blown our cover and Steve threw me a look back that said *you absolute unbelievable moron*. Steve broke the awkwardness of the situation, 'Yeah right, glove model, always the comedian. Right ladies…..who fancies a drink…', 'oh yes, that would be wonderful' came the reply and we were off walking back towards the Town centre.

The rest of the evening was uneventful. In fact, we had a good evening, having a nice meal and some drinks in a bar and then back to the hotel. I'm pretty sure our cover was blown…… but I didn't care as I've never been one for pretending to be something I'm not and at least I could now relax and be myself. There was no romance…..not for the lack of trying on Steve's part I hasten to add……but at least it ended up being an enjoyable evening. Soon enough it was time for Ingrid and Eva to catch their train back to Oslo and we escorted back to the platform. Looking back, I think Steve was also glad to bade them farewell. Once they had boarded the train Steve turned to me almost choking with laughter, 'a bloody glove model… OMG….where the hell did that come from you muppet! Come on…..let's go and have a lad's beer'. And we did.

CHAPTER 11 – PUT ME DOWN FOR A 3 BALL
Bon Jovi – Keep the Faith

Let's be really clear before we get stuck into this next episode. Steve doesn't know what sport is. It's never been something that's interested him and I dare say that he's never looked up the meaning in the Oxford English Dictionary. The idea of watching someone or a group of individuals exerting effort in chasing a ball, running down a track or rowing a boat means absolutely *diddly squat* to Steve. He'd get bored or exhausted watching it……..and within a milli-second. In many respects that has helped forge our relationship. He has no 'team allegiances', nor desire to be off down a motorway to sit with a jeering crowd. Maybe he's missing out…..maybe not? The closest Steve has come to sport is fishing…….and chasing the girls…..now that was a sport to him! So, the following account is all the stranger given his complete disinterest in sport.

I can't recall the year exactly, but it must have been the mid 1990's and during a period that Steve was briefly back in the UK between his time on the Mediterranean Cruise Ships and going to Norway. During his time in the Royal Air Force and also whilst away for 3-years on the Cruise Ships, I had developed a keen interest in Golf. After separating from a long-term girlfriend, I spent a good 3 or 4 days a week (sometimes more) playing either 9 or 18 holes. My deep-rooted interest led to me creating a Golf Society that ran for many years. During Steve's absence I'd also struck up a great relationship with his brother Neil (of toilet washing fame

– see Chapter 1), who was equally mad about playing golf and also joined the aforementioned Golf Society. We played regularly and enjoyed a beer and a social chat afterwards. It was also a nice way for me to keep in contact with Steve's family and hear of his escapades from another source (and angle!). We actually attained a pretty good standard and Neil is a great lad, really easy company. I look back fondly on those days.

Fast forward to a certain weekend in the mid 1990's and I remember visiting Steve who was now back in the UK and stopping at his parent's house in Cleveleys. Whilst there, I recall a conversation in the living room with Steve and his parents where I was waxing lyrical about the Golf Society and, in particular, about a Tournament we'd played a week earlier at which his brother Neil had won. We'd played at Ingle Golf Club and it had been a superb event with over 30 participants, fantastic weather, an abundance of prizes and a meal afterwards.

This was of course followed by a serious amount of alcohol. A blindingly good day. I think the *trigger* in Steve's head might have been on hearing how gifted his brother was at this sport and how fabulous he had been on the day in question. I also think I'd bulled Neil up so much that something snapped within those deep dark inner cogs within his brain matter. It was too much to bear.......such a gifted young brother. NOOO!!

'Right! That's it' proclaimed Steve standing up, 'where do I get one of those whackers then?', came a cry from across the living room. 'What do you mean whacker?' I replied knowing full well what he was on about. 'You know....the thingy you hit the ball with'. I think the phrase *peasant* was the first thing that came into my mind, 'If you mean the club, then that's what you use. They are NOT called whackers! There are Irons, Woods and Putters. Why….you're not thinking of having a go are you?'. 'Damn right I am' came the reply, 'if Neil and you can do it then so can I'. Puzzled. I replied with a rather furrowed brow, 'but you don't do sport…..do you'. Steve replied with exuberance, 'I don't know…..I quite like the idea of having a go at hitting a ball'. Well, this truly was a revelation, but who was I to argue? Perhaps this *might* be the one sport that Steve could enjoy. Maybe this one sport had escaped him and who knew?

'So, where do I get some clubs then' said Steve. Hmmm, this could be interesting. 'Well….I could lend you one of mine and we can go to a driving range for you to have a go'. 'No…….and what you on about driving for?'. Geez…..such a peasant, 'a driving range is a place where you can go and hit loads of golf balls, they give you in a basket full for a few quid', 'why?' came the reply, 'so you can practise and get better without causing damage or hurting someone! We can pick up some old clubs from a second-hand shop. No point in spending good money until you know whether you like it or not'. Well, I should have known what was coming, 'Nah…..take me to a shop where we can buy new gear. I don't want some second-hand rubbish!'. Before I knew it he'd donned his brown leather jacket, 'come on, let's go and get some gear. I'm looking forward to this'. I was pretty shocked at the speed of events, 'what…..right now?' I replied, 'Yep, right now…if they're still open?.

It was about 4:15pm on a Saturday and I figured if I got my foot down and got lucky with the uptown parking we might just get a few minutes in the Golf Discount Centre located in Blackpool. Before we could think sensibly on this we were in my Blue Austin Montego and driving down the promenade from Cleveleys to Blackpool.

As luck would have it, traffic was light and we got there in no time at all. We even managed to get parked only a few hundred yards away and on arriving at the store we were pleased to see that it was open until 5:30pm. Given we were only looking to buy 1 golf club I was confident that this shouldn't take too long and we'd be in and out in minutes.......or so I thought.....

We casually walked into the shop, which was very large, with an adjoining room that seemed to be even larger. This was a well-stocked place, with absolutely everything from a bag of plastic tees to remote-control golf karts. It had the lot. The shop was quiet given it was nearing closing time, and 3 bored looking sales people were strategically scattered around this super golf store. I knew the shop well enough and, *being the tight fisted one*, steered my pal Steve towards a small second-hand section near the back of the larger room, which I knew existed. This was both a genuine attempt to save Steve money and also find something suitable for a first-timer. It would also steer him away from the shop assistants eager to hit their daily sales targets towards the end of the trading day.

Just as I was picking up a good looking and reasonable priced second-hand club to show Steve, the inevitable voice broke from across the room, cutting through me like the proverbial blade in my back, 'hello there, do you need any assistance gentlemen'. No chance, was my gut reaction. We were there to buy Steve 'a' club and a cheap one at that, 'erm, no....we're ok thanks, just looking and getting ideas' I replied to the salesman. Ah ha.....that sorted him out. But then bugger lugs, somewhat predictably, broke cover, 'oh, actually, I wonder if you might help, I'd like to get kitted out for playing golf please'. My jaw dropped. Here we go again......what on earth did Steve mean 'kit me out for golf'? He'd only dreamt the idea up an hour earlier. He must have had cash burning a hole in his pocket. The sales assistant swooped in like he'd won the lottery, 'why certainly sir, was there anything in particular you were looking for'. Hmmm.....can't wait to hear this one I thought. 'Well. I've not played before so I'm not looking for anything top range, something in-between would be fine' came the reply from Steve. Agh, sweet......at least he was telling the truth. I interjected, 'yeah, he hasn't a clue basically and he's just looking for 1 club so he can get a feel for it down at the driving range'. Steve looked across at me with distain, 'no, I am not after one, I want as many as you're allowed. I want a full set of the thingies'. Oh, sweet Jesus' mother of Mary......did he have any idea how much this lot was going to cost him! The salesman's eyes glistened, his comrades moving in to get a piece of the action. 'Great. Well, may I recommend these mid-range clubs we have on offer, reduced to £399 for the set'. Ok, I put my hand up. I coughed out loud at this point in shock and disgust, earning me an indifferent look from both the sales team and Steve, 'you ok there McAttack', 'erm, yes, something stuck in my throat'.

The sales team went into overdrive and Steve was lapping it up like a kitten taking milk from it's mother. 'Well sir, that's the clubs sorted, you'll be wanting a matching bag, 'well, hell yes, I've always wanted a matching golf bag', came the reply, 'and a putter, drivers, golf balls, tees, golf shoes, sweater, water proofs etc etc'. You get the gist. I may have missed something but it took the extra sales staff and myself to help carry all this clobber to the till.

The receipt was massive. I've no idea what the bill came to

but it must have been circa £1,000. Don't forget this was the mid-1990's and that was a lot of money back then! I have absolutely no idea how someone can go from 'wanting to have a go at hitting a golf ball', to purchasing the full monty within the hour. Absolutely bonkers.

Even worse he now had better golf equipment than myself!! He had so much gear (all new and in huge boxes) that I had to go and fetch the car and bring it right up to the front of the shop, which was located on a very busy road taking traffic outside Blackpool Town Centre. Needless to say, we managed to get the car loaded and get Steve home to his parent's house.

His mum Val opened the door having seen us wrestling up the driveway with umpteen cardboard boxes, 'what on earth have you been buying, not sure I've got room for all that'? I interjected, 'well we went to buy 'a' golf club and he ended up buying the bloody shop'. Cue puzzled look from mum, 'but you don't even like sport. Let alone Golf'? Steve, was full of beans, 'well I do now don't I....see look what I have mother'. Geez....the unpredictable one had struck again! At least the cash burning a hole in his pocket had been put to good use.

Having unpacked I suggested it was time for me to head off home for dinner, 'right Steve, I'll be in touch tomorrow. We can get up to the driving range at Bispham and try this clobber out'. Clearly, having bought the gear Steve thought he was immediately the next Nick Faldo, 'driving range. Nah. Sod that. I want to get on a golf course like you and Neil.
Get us lined up for a golf course somewhere tomorrow and, in fact, call my brother and invite him. Put us down for a three ball'. Where on earth had he picked that up from!! Must have read something in the shop. This was all now causing me major concern, 'hang on Steve, you need to get some practise

in first. It can be bloody dangerous golf. You need to learn how to hit the ball first'. He wasn't having any of it, 'screw that. Just get us sorted out. I'll be right. Can't wait. See you tomorrow. Bye'. And the door shut. Here we go again, mad man Redman strikes……this time with a shiny new set of golf clubs!

On reaching home I called Poulton Golf Club (no mobile phone back then), a small privately owned 9-hole course that was suitable for a new starter. However, I ensured that I booked a tee-off time much later in the day, when I knew the course would be quiet and a safer environment for everyone. I then called his brother Neil. 'Hi Neil, it's Greg. You fancy a game of golf tomorrow evening around 5pm, just 9 holes at Poulton'?. Neil seemed pleased I had called, 'I don't see why not. Sounds good to me. Stick me down'. 'Great. Nice one Neil. Just one other thing. Your brother is playing a three ball with us'. There then followed a few seconds silence, 'Excuse me?…… but he doesn't even like sport. Let alone Golf'?

No time for explanation, dinner was nearly ready, 'Yep. Well, he's only just gone out and bought bloody everything. And I mean everything'…….'Jesus'…….came the reply. 'I'll see you tomorrow around 4:30pm in the carpark'. A stunned Neil gave an equally short reply, 'err….ok…see you then…bye'.

The next day was a beautiful summers day. I can't recall what I did in the daytime but by mid-afternoon I was enroute to collect Cleveleys new Seve Ballesteros. On reaching Steve's I tapped the front door, which was swiftly opened by the boy wonder, 'what you reckon to this McAttack'. Heart attack time. From somewhere the clown had found a polo neck sweater and V-neck jumper. Catalogue Ken golf attire 1974 had just landed. 'Oh, my God. Not sure I want to be seen anywhere near you. That wasn't cool in the decade it came out', 'ah ha.....jealousy will get you nowhere. Come on then, I'm ready to go'.

We loaded up the car with his new golf equipment, his clubs now loaded into his new golf bag, and drove the short 15minute drive to Poulton Golf Club. On arriving at the golf club carpark his brother Neil was stood there tending to his clubs that he'd just unloaded from his own car, cigarette dangling from his lip. I swear that cigarette nearly went for a burton as his jaw dropped on seeing his brother, 'Oh, my God. Did you get that clobber from the back of Dad's wardrobe? That wasn't cool in the decade it came out!'. 'Oh, shut up you old tart. That's what he said', pointing to myself, 'what do you girls know about golf fashion anyway, I mean look at you peasants. No class or style.

Now come along boys....we've a match to play', as our novice strode off. Oh, why oh why do I get myself into these scrapes with Redman, I thought to myself. We saddled up our golf bags to their trolleys, paid our fees to the nice man at the Club shop and made our way to the first tee.

It was a beautiful evening. The sun had dropped but there wasn't a breath of wind and it was in fact a perfect evening for golf. Even better there was nobody else to be seen. I think we were quite literally the only people out on the course......well apart from the odd rabbit that were now making their way onto the edges of the fairways to graze.

The first tee at Poulton was a very short Par 3 (3 attempts to get the ball in the hole). There wasn't a chance he could do much damage here. And I was right. On hitting his shot it barely left the ground and rolled much of the way towards the green. Indeed, it is such a short hole that he wasn't far off the green. 'What did I do wrong? I wanted it to go up in the air like yours and Neil's? I want to do that!'….came the cry from the petulant child. 'Well…..I did tell you we should have gone on the driving range…..but would you listen to me……..as per usual NO'. Off we trundled towards our golf balls where we were able to put our shots in with varying degrees of success but with no issues. I don't think any of us faired too badly on that first hole.

Next up was a long but narrow Par 4. Straight as an arrow to the green but a tight fairway and a large out of bounds farmers field off to the right. We agreed that Steve should go first so Neil and myself could *analyse* his golf swing. However, this fairway also had a public footpath on the right, leading in from a local housing estate. As Steve was teeing up his ball a lady, maybe in her early fifties, emerged from the side entrance near the housing estate with her Golden Retriever dog. Neil interjected, 'best we wait until she's a way down there Steve', 'yeah. No problem. Best to wait', came Steve's reply.

The 3 of us stood there watching the dog walker walking away from us, whilst Steve performed warm-up stretching exercises with his driver.

The first hole had gone pretty well all things considered. I was with my best pals, on a beautiful summers evening with a golf course to ourselves and no doubt a few beers waiting at the end. My mind wandered and I thought that perhaps, just maybe, I was wrong and that Steve could learn this sport and it become something we could do together as a hobby going forward?

I'm not sure how far the lady had gotten, but she must have been around 130 -150 yards away. 'I think you'll be OK now Steve, she's a way off. You'd be lucky to get near her' said his brother Neil. 'Eye eye cap 'ain' came the reply from Steve who initially checked his ball and then steadied himself for the shot. Neil and myself stood to the right of him in silence, hands resting on our drivers. Steve Looked the part he did. A natural. An A-Team player primed to go. Then, like all new golfers, he went for absolute power and swung his club like the proverbial axeman at the chopping block. He gave it absolutely everything. Steve is a well-built unit and has always been very strong…..and he was coming in on that ball hammer and tongue! If he misses the ball, his arm is coming out of its socket! However, all seasoned players know that golf is about finesse….and those beginners who try to clobber everything only get lucky shots every now and then and, over time, they learn to curb it. Maybe beginner's luck was about to kick in……..?

What happened next is imprinted on my brain. I shall not forget it until the day I die. It is there, stuck in my memory bank forevermore. Steve hit the ball with absolute venom. One of the most powerful shots I've ever seen from anyone. He also hit it as sweet as a nut and as straight as an arrow…..but the problem being he wasn't looking straight down the fairway when he hit it. Instead, he hit it straight towards the dog walker. The ball accelerated at a ridiculous speed but it never got more than 4ft above in the air. It screamed over the ground at an unprecedented pace. It was heading right for the lady in question, honing in like an Exocet missile, nothing was going to stop it. 'Oooh, hey, err…..what do you shout…..what do they say, what do they say'? Steve was scrambling for the word *Fore* the warning to anyone on a golf course that a ball is coming in close to them. But it was too late. The ball slammed into the small of the ladies back so hard that it took her out completely. A foot higher and it would have been the back of her head; I dread to think.

I shall never forget the sight of her flailing arms, exactly as you see in war movies when a soldier gets shot. Steve had completely and utterly taken her out ...her feet fully off the floor. She hit the ground like a sack of potatoes, and lay slumped on the ground. It was bad. On a scale of badness from 1-10....this was a 12. 'Oh, crap'...shouted Steve who was now off down the fairway in his 1970's golf attire, running to tend to the poor lady, leaving his golf clubs and paraphernalia behind. I was shocked and Neil too. We were regulars at this Golf Club and didn't want to be seen anywhere near Steve or be associated with him. We were off. Pronto. I'm ashamed to say we scarpered back towards the Club House carpark. My equipment was in the boot of my car before anyone could shout Jack Frost.....and so was Neil's. 'Oh my god', said Neil, 'we never should have brought him. Oh bloody hell we'll be banned' etc etc. We nearly beat it......but decided to wait and see if the emergency services arrived or not. After 15-20 minutes Steve *Ballistic* Redman came round the corner of the Clubhouse.....not looking quite so cocky. 'Oh my God Steve....you took that lady out. You absolute idiot. Is she ok'? Steve looked pretty Sheepish, 'Yeah she's ok. I think it was more of the shock. I tried to pick her up and she started shouting at me "*get off me, get off me* you idiot". I don't think I caused any damage.....think it was more of a shock really'.

Neil and myself breathed a sigh of relief. 'Hey.....are we having a beer in the Clubhouse?' enquired Steve, 'no we're bloody not! That'll get back to the staff in there and we're regulars…..don't want them knowing we were with you! That lady might come back too!'. Steve looked at us apologetically, 'fair enough…… maybe enough for a first outing. Always time for a cheeky one in the Sandpiper though'. 'Come on then' I replied.

Just before jumping into our cars Steve asked, 'hey lads, either of you interested in buying a full set of golf clubs…..barely used……………'.

CHAPTER 12 – THE EAGLE HAS COLLIDED!
Oasis – Rock N' Roll Star

Our early teens saw the dynamic duo strive to become accomplished Ice Skaters. We frequented the Blackpool Ice Arena at Blackpool Pleasure Beach perhaps a little too often, when homework and study might have been more pressing given we were heading towards our GCSE examinations. But we grew up in Blackpool, the UK's Las Vegas. With its bright lights and a vibrant night life, Blackpool was at the far end of the spectrum on the excitement Richter-Scale compared to many of the hum drum Towns and villages up and down the Country. Indeed, it often crossed our minds *what on earth do they do round here to entertain themselves (?)* when visiting some more remote parts of the UK. The distractions were aplenty in Blackpool.

The highlight of the skating week was *Beat Night* at Blackpool Pleasure Beach's Ice Arena. Steve would catch the Tram from Cleveleys and I'd hop on at Gynn Square, North Shore Blackpool, for the remainder of the journey along the Promenade to South Shore Blackpool. Beat Night provided a high octane mix of disco and ice skating and a place to meet and impress the ladies.

The *Mad Dash* was called by the resident DJ an hour or so into the evening, a cue for those of lesser skating ability to vacate the rink, leaving those who were either fool hardy, or with exceptional talent, to *strut their stuff* so to speak. Over time both of us attained a pretty competent level of Ice skating. Of course, you'll have gathered already that Steve has an inbuilt trigger to outperform yours truly and thus it wasn't uncommon to see Steve skating backwards in the Mad Dash. Incredibly brave. But also incredibly stupid. The man excels at being the idiot in such environments! This *hell for leather* scramble at break neck speeds under astonishing bright strobe lights saw more than its fair share of participants crash and burn, some suffering injury. However, apart from the occasional fall or tumble I don't recall either of us encountering anything other than the odd bruise. God only knows how.

I must admit that Steve nudged it when it came to skating ability, always the daredevil, although by some margin I faired rather better with the ladies at the rink. Of course, he will dispute that! Naturally Steve always endeavoured to scupper my chances, 'rough as toast pal', 'smells terrible that girl, didn't you notice', 'I'm doing you a favour pulling you away from her….trust me'. He was, metaphorically, the big St. Bernard coming to my rescue……..which of course I didn't need or want! Maybe he did save me. Who knows? Suffice to say by the time we had reached our mid-teens we were both accomplished skaters and, without question, we had many happy hours at the ice-rink. It was great fun and fantastic socialising.

Fast forward a few years and Steve was now settled in Norway with his long-term girlfriend Ellen, destined to become his future wife. Steve was eager that my own girlfriend Mel (also destined to become my wife) and myself should come over for a week of fun in the snow and, for the first time in our lives, go skiing. Naturally we couldn't wait. Norway is a stunning country, clean and crisp with amazing scenery. I also find the Norwegians great people, always hospitable and welcoming. They are also extremely organised and share the Brits sense of humour and outlook on life.

I had visited Norway several times prior to this trip for the odd weekend but more often than not in the summer months. So, there was a degree of excitement as Mel and myself headed off to C&A to get kitted out in his and her ski apparel.

For the younger generation, C&A was a well-known national Department Store that was known for its Ski clothing. Alas it went bankrupt quite a few years ago in the UK, although I note that it still trades in other European countries such as Germany at the point of writing.

The holiday soon arrived and Mel and myself escaped from work for a week of fun in the snow. We flew British Airways to Oslo's Gardermoen Airport, located north of the city, where Steve was there to greet us. Excitement was in the air as we drove for another 1.5 hrs north to the small but expanding Town of Elverum in the Hedmark region of Norway. Being in our 20's and no children, it didn't take long before the beers were flowing at Steve and Ellen's house in the old part of Elverum.

Indeed, their house was very old, made of wood with low ceilings and beams, which you inevitably cracked your head on at least twice on each visit. The roof was covered in turf with wild grass, acting as insulation from the harsh winters that Norway endures each year. In fact, it wasn't uncommon for temperatures to hit -20 during our visits. This wasn't the French Alps! The Norwegian are a tardy bunch and no wonder. Steve proclaimed with much gusto that we were scheduled to leave early the next morning for Trysil, one of Norway's premier Ski Resorts and approximately an hour away. The town of Elverum is in fact situated approximately

1hour from Trysil and also Lillehammer, the largest Ski Resort in Norway and of Olympic fame. It is no accident (pardon the pun) that Elverum has one of Norway's largest Orthopaedic Hospital units complete with Helicopter landing pad! I guess that is primarily for the Tourists.....because they say the Norwegian is born with *skis on their feet*. As a Nation they are accomplished at this activity and children often ski to school in the long winter months.

After a good night's sleep, and only a minimal hangover from the previous evenings drinking, the four of us set off in the car for Trysil. Enroute, and only a couple of miles outside Elverum, Steve pointed eagerly to a Ski jump, as of Eddie the Eagle fame, proclaiming, 'you ain't seen nothing yet McAttack.........wait until you see the one we've lined up for you'. Hmm. Always the wind-up merchant.....or was he? I was certainly starting to get a little nervous.

Finally, we arrived at Trysil and it did not disappoint. The weather was perfect, an azure blue sky, with not a cloud to be seen. The sun was beating down and we could quite easily have been in the Alps. I'd clocked a huge trampoline whilst driving in, with people practising summersaults. I had a feeling that the calibre of those on the slopes was going to be infinitely higher than that of Mel and myself and we were going to feel out of place. However, Steve had assured us that we'd be straight onto the nursery slope for some practise.

Once checked in at reception and already kitted out in our new C&A ski clothing, we proceeded to get boots and skis hired. Steve and Ellen had their own, so once Mel and myself were kitted out we were ready to go. The resort was busy and who could blame so many people turning out on this prize of a day. It was apparent that the vast majority of skiers were Norwegian, although we did meet some fellow Brits and noted some other nationalities.

The nursery slope was right at the bottom of the Trysilfjellet mountain, from which all ski runs descended, and so we all grabbed the basic ski lift that soon had us at the top of this gentle slope.
Like myself, Mel was a good Ice Skater and was fairly confident that she would be ok. Mel had also frequented the Pleasure Beach Ice Arena in her teens, although being younger it was a few years after Steve and myself. And so it proved to be that Steve's claim that you could skate if you could ski was correct. The bend in the knees and means of turning was, in principle, pretty similar.....at least I thought so. It was decided that Ellen would accompany Mel down the slope and Steve myself, so off we set. We both successfully navigated our way to the bottom with no issues and I recall we both thoroughly enjoyed the experience. Smiles all round. Good friends, a world class Ski Resort and a stunning day. A day to live for. We proceeded to do the nursery run for another hour and our confidence was growing after each run; it's safe to say that we were enjoying the experience.

From here on in the story rather takes a turn for the worse. On reaching the bottom of perhaps my 15th run on the nursery slope Steve suggested that Mel stay with Ellen and practise further whilst we proceeded to another level. 'Are you sure Steve, we've not been on this one that long and we do have the rest of the day still'? 'Blah, of course. You're doing bloody fantastic pal so methinks you're ready for a change in scenery', said Steve with aplomb. Mel was content to stay with Ellen, advising it was 'up to me' if I went onto the next stage. I was still unconvinced.

However, before I could dwell on this too long Steve announced that the pair of us were off to achieve something greater. I remonstrated one last time, 'Steve.......we've been here an hour, I've never skied before and I'd rather practise some more on the nursey slope along with Mel'. Steve declared with much gusto that I was a *wuss* and to shut up and follow him. 'Trust me, I'm your best mate', he ventured. Momentarily I thought of staying put with Mel and Ellen, surely he wouldn't do anything stupid? But I didn't like the *wuss* label so, with some trepidation I bade farewell to Mel and Ellen and trotted off after him.

We soon arrived at a much larger Ski lift, complete with seating for multiple persons. There didn't seem to be too many folk on this one, so we managed to jump on a carriage just to ourselves. The lift ride was thoroughly brilliant, as it went higher and higher the views across the Hedmark region were spectacular. After a while the height from the ground grew and became alarmingly high! 'Where the hell are we going Steve' I asked now starting to panic, 'to the top McAttack', said Steve with a mischievous chuckle. I wanted to kill him.

Why would someone do such a thing to a complete novice? 'What, to the top? You better not be taking me anywhere near a black run'. Steve gave a wry smirk and I knew straight away that he'd gone beyond any prank he'd EVER played before! But I was committed, there was no way off the carriage, although it's fair to say that the mood became a little contemplative. Finally, we reached the top. Alarmingly there weren't too many Skiers at the *final destination*. There were no happy families here having fun in the snow. No loving couples holding hands. No, here at the summit there was a decidedly more serious sense of affairs. The Skiers here definitely hadn't been shopping at C&A and the resort assistants looked rather more serious and sterner. The sun-drenched lower slopes were way beneath us now. Up here the sun was screened by the summit of Trysilfjellet and the temperature was truly Baltic. I had a Commercial Airliner Pilots view of Norway and my heart rate was extremely high as I stood trembling on a narrow icy ledge. Interestingly, I noted that the witty one was not looking so clever with himself now and, if I was able to read his mind, I'm pretty sure he was thinking, 'hmm, maybe not my greatest idea'. Even though he was a good skier, this was a place for the accomplished and not the faint hearted!

We shuffled along the ledge towards the drop zone. It felt incredibly narrow and my vertigo was kicking in. I had a new found respect for Eddie the Eagle! I watched those who had arrived before us disappear into the abyss, one by one. Nearer and nearer we got to the starting point which was being supervised by a huge rather serious looking Norwegian. You wouldn't want to argue with him. Steve was chuckling away to himself the whole time, having found his black sense of humour again.

And then, there it was. The sign that told me I was at the highest point in the Ski Resort and, devastatingly for me, it was a Black Run! Here was Greg, from North Shore Blackpool, proficient Ice Skater and with 1 hour on a Nursery slope under his belt stood looking down a near vertical descent, kitted out in his C&A finest and bobble hat. Even the few Norwegians up there were thinking twice before throwing themselves off the edge. But they were suitably equipped. They looked like they were being filmed for Ski Sunday in their body-hugging ski-suits and crash helmets! They'd spent a life honing their skiing skills to take on such challenges.

I, on the other hand, was definitely NOT ready for this. This was ridiculous, mind bendingly crazy and I hated Steve for it! 'I can't do it; I need to get the lift back down' I pleaded to Steve. I'm not sure what was funny, but Steve was bent double laughing, 'you're kacking your knickers' came the cry in between bouts of laughter. Damn right I was. I was enjoying life and this was a sure way of ending it! After slightly composing himself Steve advised that 'you can't get the lift back down, you're not allowed. The only way down is to ski'. 'Well, get them to fetch one of those snowmobiles up here' I demanded. 'Can't. They don't come up this far, too steep', came the reply. I stood there, shocked and to be frank rather upset. I was also freezing and petrified. I'd been in some scrapes with Steve before but this was the daddy of them all. Give me a cop chase round Cleveleys any day of the week. This was complete and utter lunacy.

However, I realised the die was cast and I really did have no option. I contemplated sliding on my bottom but considered that 1) I'd look ridiculous, 2) I could become a danger / hazard for other skiers and 3) it would probably take me 2hrs to get from top to bottom when all I wanted was for it to be over!

I'm not sure where I managed to get the mental strength but I just went, catching Steve off guard. I didn't think. I just went – GO!!! I can only suppose that an innate trigger decided *don't dwell on this.* People who have done a parachute or bungee jump for the first time might understand that inexplicable internal power that almost possesses your body and makes you do something that you didn't think you could. But I was off and the slope was terrifyingly steep and the soft powdery snow on the lower slopes was not to be found here. Up at these lofty heights it was rather icier, making this much more treacherous.

I decided rather quickly that in order to avert certain death, I needed to slow the pace by putting in as many turns as possible to zig zag down the mountain. This seemed to be doing the trick, but I was going at one hell of a pace and thus the turns were coming thick and fast. It was exhausting. On more than one occasion I nearly lost it in the turn; but so far I was hanging in there and I raced down the slope hundreds of metres in no time at all. Miraculously I was holding it together and better still the gradient of the slope seemed to be easing and the ariel view across Hedmark disappearing. My confidence started to rise, but only a little.

Now, suddenly, way in the distance I could make out buildings, the small cluster of resort hotels. I felt I was nearing safety. And thus, whilst the slope was still horrendously steep, I threw caution to the wind, I quit putting in the turns and threw the skis poles under my arms, tucked them up tight, knees closer together and head down hell for leather. I'd seen the professionals do this in the Winter Olympics and was convinced that this was a sure way of ending this drama as quickly as possible. Being a tad heavier than my side-kick I was soon propelling down the slope at breakneck speed.

The undulations on the slope were playing havoc on my thighs, which were acting as shock absorbers! I have no idea what speed I reached, but it must surely have been in excess of 60 miles per hour plus? A quick glance over my shoulder told me that I had left Steve for dust and I was hurtling towards the finish line, pine trees flickered past me at an alarming rate.

I managed to make a dogleg turn at a terrific speed and was feeling rather pleased with myself but then, maybe 1000 yards ahead of me I saw a sight I shall never forget. There, in the distance, but growing ever closer was a Ski School!!

A novice group neatly in a row cutting across the slope in a chain, following their Instructor like ducklings following their mother. Maybe 15 people of all age groups being led to another slope. It was not lost on me after the event that I probably should have been in that group!

There is no question, absolutely none, that at the rate I was travelling at I was going to seriously hurt someone, perhaps even kill people as the way they were spread across the slope I just couldn't see a way through. In fact the problem was threefold; 1) it was a particularly narrow section of the run, 2) the Ski School had spread out right across the run and I could see no way through and 3) I didn't have the knowhow of stopping at such a speed. I therefore made a split-second decision to deliberately fall over. I knew I may hurt if not kill myself. But it was the only means of not ending up in court on a manslaughter charge! I therefore threw myself down to my left-hand side.

What happened next is quite literally a blur. An explosion of snow, a feeling of tumbling, turning over and over. My Ski Poles gone in an instance, one ski came off, continued to tumble and slide. Then the other Ski was gone. Continuing to roll the world spinning. Then breaking of branches and a loud *crush* noise as I slammed into a small fern tree at some speed. No motion. Silence. Apart from my breath and the pounding of my heart there was nothing. Just the sun glinting off the snow, my eyes straining having also lost my goggles.

All was tranquil and beautiful. My body was contorted and I lay momentarily, nature and physics having combined to deposit me unceremoniously into that tree. Am I hurt, have I broken anything? No! Nothing, no pain whatsoever. Quite remarkably I had survived without so much as a bruise. Furthermore, the Ski School was gone, and none the wiser for the averted tragedy! I sat up, pleased that the escapade was over and I had survived unscathed. Quite astonished to be in one piece if the truth be known. Having come to my senses and established I was completely unhurt, I realised that most of my *hired* equipment was nowhere to be seen. I had 1 ski pole and that was it. My immediate thoughts in the aftermath were what a ruddy pain it was going to be to find it all!

At that moment Steve arrived, turning sharply to come to an abrupt Stop. He looked at me for a split second and then, having realised that I was unhurt, bent double laughing. He was laughing so hard, he could barely breathe, tears rolling down his face.

Steve likes to laugh and it's fair to say there have been plenty of belly laughs down the years…..but this one sticks in the memory. He was laughing that hard he quite literally nearly passed out. He had seen it all from some 800 meters behind. 'Oh….. my…….. god!'….he proclaimed, 'you lost it big time, an explosion of snow engulfed you' he shouted in between the tears and laughing. 'Lost it!!!! I lost nothing! My act was purely in the interests of saving others!'. I was outraged!! This wasn't a moment for being ridiculed……..I should be getting a gallantry medal for such an act of valour! In the face of incredible adversity 'I' had saved the day. But Steve hadn't seen the Ski School and wasn't hearing a word of it 'poor excuse' came the reply, 'let's face it McAttack, you lost it', 'what

Ski School……can't see anything of the sort'. Redman was surely having a laugh. I'd only learnt to Ski one hour earlier!! But then I also saw the funny side and started laughing too. It had been an incredibly stupid act to take me to the top of that black run, but we have survived once again, unscathed and would live to tell the tale. How on earth I hadn't at least broken a bone I'll never know.

There had been too much drama for one day and we were done. Eventually Steve helped me to my feet, took off his own Ski's and we then spent 20 minutes retrieving my equipment, which was strewn all over the place. One Ski landing 5 feet up in a tree! Remarkably we did find all the equipment, it hadn't taken as long as I'd feared and, even better, nothing appeared to be damaged.

Having put all my equipment back on we skied together the short distance back to the bottom of the slope together, which was now much gentler. Soon enough, we reached the end of the ski run and spotted our betrothed waiting for us…… complete with stern faces and folded arms. Hmm…..the arms folded thing is always a dead giveaway. 'Where the hell have you two been? Thought you'd left us for the day' said Ellen, 'you've been gone for ages', said Mel glaring at myself. Geez……if only they knew! 'Agh, stop your squarking' said Steve, 'come tither, follow me. time for drinky poos'……and the 4 intrepid skiers disappeared together down the slope for some lunchtime après ski, our secret safe for the time being!

CHAPTER 13 – I'M HIS BEST MATE…..DOCTOR!
Robbie Williams – Kids

Having a friend live in Norway was great. I visited often over the 15 or so years Steve lived there, sometimes on my own and sometimes with Mel who at the time was my girlfriend. They were often short trips over a long weekend and served as an opportunity to catch-up with Steve and Ellen. I really like the Norwegians – I find their outlook on life and sense of humour very similar to that of the British - and visiting different places was always great fun. Oslo, Elverum, Trysil, Kristiansand, Bergen and Rjukan to name a few, the latter being famous for the war film Heroes of Telemark, starring Kirk Douglas.

Best of all I enjoyed the winter snow. You will have read earlier about our exploits at the Ski Resort at Trysil and here we have another story involving winter sports, but not in Trysil this time. It wasn't always necessary to travel to an expensive resort to enjoy the winter snow.

Mel and I would, on occasions, just jump on a budget airways flight to Sandefjord (south of Oslo) and then get a bus to Elverum where Steve and Ellen lived and venture out to various places nearby such as Budor, which is a small ski location well off the tourist destination list.

However, this escapade concerns a visit to Steve and Ellen's house in Elverum, with no plan other than to stay local and catch-up. We'd agreed to pop over for a long weekend with some mutual friends, James, Paula and their Son Alexander

(Ali). Steve assured us that there had been heavy snowfall in the town of Elverum and that the hill, at the end of the road where they lived, was superb and in fine condition for sledging. A few beers, a bit of a social catch-up and a bit of sledging suited us just fine, although there was also the prospect of a trip to Budor too. Given there were a few of us this time and also given it was a short visit, we decided to fly from Manchester to the main Airport at Gardermoen and then catch a bus to Elverum.

A few years earlier and the flight would have taken us into Oslo's main International Airport at Fornebu, very close to the city. However, the powers that be decided to redevelop a military airport north of Oslo at Gardermoen but put in place a high-speed rail link connection to Oslo city centre. Fornebu finally closed on 7 October 1998 as it just didn't have the space for expansion and plus it was considered a little too close to the city for heavy commercial aircraft. However, Gardermoen was actually nearer to Steve and Ellen's home town of Elverum, just over an hour away, which was a bonus. In addition, it would appear no expense was spared on the Gardermoen Terminal, which is stunning and very Scandinavian in design. So, there would be good duty-free shopping on the return leg! Don't forget Norway was and still is outside the European Economic Union……. something else we now have in common with the Norwegians post Brexit! So, a duty-free haul was always in order on the return leg!

Everyone was a bit giddy and really looking forward to the weekend. The travel arrangements went without a hitch, from being picked up by the Taxi at home and delivered to Manchester Airport, to the flight and then bus journey once in Norway. Being an aviation enthusiast, I always treasured the flights into Norwegian Airspace, coming along their South Coast and over places like Kristiansand, the location of another one of the likely lads exploits!!

Of course, it wasn't always clear and I didn't always get a window seat, but when the stars aligned and I did, it was amazing owing to the stunning scenery. Norway is one of the most frequented countries I've been too, perhaps after Germany, which I visited a significant number of times through work.

On landing at Gardermoen Steve was there to greet us, 'Yo Party People Wasup!!'. Clearly the dude was up for a party. 'Right, here's the plan. With Ali being a child, I'll take Ali and Paula (mum) in my car with some of the luggage and scoot on ahead, whilst you 3 get the bus. By the time I've dropped them off at my house the bus should be nearing Elverum, so I'll come over to the bus terminal to pick you guys up. Trust that's ok for everyone'. Indeed it was and so we split with the intention of meeting up in an hour or so. Mel, James and myself boarded the correct bus without any trouble and sat back to enjoy the journey through the beautiful and sparsely populated countryside. Forest, lakes and fjords for miles, simply stunning.

I always remember the ride alongside Lake Mjøsa towards Hamar. The lake is huge in length and always seemed endless - ever present as we headed north.
And Steve was right, there was a significant amount of snow everywhere. Of course, the Norwegians are well setup to deal with the snowfall and the roads were clear, although all vehicles require special tyres from around November onwards.

Eventually we arrived at the bus Terminal in Elverum and Steve true to his word was waiting for us. However, given the amount of luggage he kindly did a couple of shuttle runs from the bus terminal in the centre of the town to his log-cabin house on the other side of the town but not too far away. Steve drove Mel over first with the luggage and James and myself waited for the second collection.....women, children and luggage first!

On arriving at Steve's house we were met by Ellen, Steve's girlfriend (future wife), and there was a real buzz in the air, 'great to see you guys, come on in!' as we were met with a warm embrace. The log fire was already raging and a lovely warmth radiating throughout the house. The house was very old, one of the oldest properties in the town, with low wooden beams, especially the ones upstairs, which I never failed to whack my head on at least once during each visit!

By the time James and myself had hung up our winter coats in the vestibule and kicked off our thick hiking boots, the beer and wine was already flowing. Excited chatter could be heard throughout the house as people caught up with one another. In fact, the beer and wine was probably going down too well and between us we were guzzling it away like it were going out of fashion! We'd only been there an hour and I think we were all feeling the effects.

Steve was making a Corn beef hash, having managed to source some, something Ellen had never tried before. 'Eh....McAttack.......watch this.....I'm going to get Ellen.....she's never had corned beef before'. Steve had chopped up a tin of corned beef on a board in the kitchen. I wasn't sure where he was going with this. 'Ellen, Ellen....can

I borrow you for a minute'. Not only did Ellen arrive in the kitchen but so did Mel, James and Paula, charged glasses in hand. 'Here, Ellen, try some of this and let me know what you think?' as he passed her a chunk of corned beef. Ellen looked at it sheepishly, 'what is it' as she held it between her fingers thinking twice before going any further, 'It's nice, trust me, just give it a go', said Steve with a degree of sincerity. Ellen popped the chunk of corned beef in her mouth and started to chew whilst grimacing, 'what the hell is it' she said with real concern.

Cue Steve's announcement, 'it's cat food you plonker!', 'oh my god' came the shout as she spat it into the kitchen bin and frantically raced to the sink to wash her mouth out between cries of, 'you bastard, you bastard, why would you do that'.

The onlookers were creased and an explosion of laughter filled the kitchen. Once composed, Steve put her mind at rest, whilst wiping tears of laughter from his face, 'we're only kidding. It's called corned beef, it's not cat food. You can eat it. It's popular in the UK'. Ellen shrugged her shoulder looking a little relieved, 'are you guys sure'? 'yes, yes of course' came the replies from the watching crowd. 'You're still a git though Redman', came her retort. And who could blame her!

It was at that point that the doorbell rang and a voice could be heard as the vestibule inner door swung open, 'hello'. It was Ellen's sister Sysil with her son and daughter Mari and Evan, who were young kids. They were off to the hill to sledge and wanted to know if Ali wanted to go sledging too? 'Well, I think we should all go. Why don't we all get down there for a bit before it goes dark. What do you all think?' said Steve. I think it's fair to say that the decision was unanimous, with several 'hell yeah's' being heard across the living room.

Within a few minutes everyone was trying to get re-kitted out in their winter gear all crammed into the vestibule. It was like a scene from a Griswold's family outing, with cries of 'where's my other boot' and 'where did I put my gloves?'. Eventually the semi-inebriated gang were outdoors and heading off down the icy road towards the hill at the end of the road. It was bloody freezing, maybe -10, but this was the life and with rosy cheeks and much excitement the tribe marched off towards the hill with a couple of sledges that Steve and Ellen had.

The hill wasn't far away, maybe 800 metres. When we arrived, there were a few other local children having fun on the slope. It was of reasonable size and gradient and was treelined at the top. 'What's that' I said to Steve pointing to a huge mound at the bottom of the slope and next to the quiet road that the slope ran onto. 'Basically, every time the snow plough comes down the road it pushes all the snow to the side and after weeks and months it builds up and up into a huge mound. It gets like that every year after heavy snowfall', 'ah, OK' I replied. Sysil's kids were already on their way up the slope as was Ali and his mum Paula. Sysil turned to us, 'everyone needs to be careful, the slope is quite compact and icy', 'oh don't worry we will be careful' I replied. Hmmm…..famous last words…

Having let the children have a go for a while and then having watched most of the adults have a go, I proclaimed with much gusto that it was my turn next, 'right…..come on James, pass me that sledge….time for McAttack to show you how it's done', I said acutely aware that the alcohol effects had kicked in and I was feeling a little stupefied. The sledge in question wasn't a traditional sledge, but rather a round plastic bin lid design but with handles to hold on to. I had noted, whilst observing the others, that whilst it looked great fun, there was zero control compared to a traditional sledge where you could lean left or right to turn. This thing seemed to spin folk round and around on their way to the bottom. But is seemed faster and more dangerous so obviously that was the ride of choice!

With bright red plastic sledge in hand, I trudged to the top of the hill. Despite the cold it got my heart rate going sure enough, the alcohol intake didn't seem like such a good idea anymore. Despite not being a particularly high hill, given the comparatively flatness of Elverum, it provided a pretty good view across the town. I recall Ali and his mum were on the more traditional wooden sledge next to me, 'It's too fast that thing for Ali, we're going to stick with this I think' said Paula. 'I understand. Watch this, I'm going to bomb it down'.

And with that I threw myself onto the circular sledge, managing to get into a sitting position first time and successfully grabbing the handles either side firmly. The sledge accelerated at an alarming speed, the manner in which I had thrown myself onto it ensuring that I got away to a blistering start. Even worse the thing was spinning me around and around like a crazy Wurlitzer ride at a fairground. I was in danger of taking out anyone else in my way but fortunately by now there were only a few people left on the slope. The speed grew and grew at an alarming rate and in no time I was hell for leather!

I was now nearing the bottom at terrific speed but the whoops and hollering from Steve, Ellen, Mel and James soon stopped when I shot past them, all stood in a place where most folks ride ends! Instead, I shot on towards the road, still not slowing down. There were no cars coming but I was heading towards the snow mound as created by the snow plough. I wasn't overly concerned and expected a soft impact. Instead, I got the shock of my life. Whilst the snow mound was covered in nice soft snow, underneath had become compact ice over many weeks and months. I slammed smack into the mound on my right-hand side. I was in instant agony, feeling like I'd been flung into a brick wall. I was in severe pain in my right leg and I knew straight away that I'd really hurt myself. I couldn't move. I could however hear the drunken crowd crying themselves with laughter.

Aside from obviously looking rather amusing to them, they probably thought I was playing the fool lying ridged on the floor. But I wasn't. I was in excruciating pain and I was sure I'd broken my leg. I'd broken an ankle, ribs, wrist and a finger in the past….so I knew what pain that brought, and this was similar. The Griswold's posse eventually walked over realising that I had actually hurt myself. 'Come on McAttack. Let's stick you on the wooden sledge and all go home. Probably just a dead-leg so stop your whinging. Besides its going dark and we've got that corned beef hash still to eat'. And so, James and Steve gingerly lifted me onto the sledge, which was more painful than they'll ever realise!

The walk, or in my case sledge ride, to Steve and Ellen's house was a short one, but I don't recall it and cared for nothing as my entire being was consumed by the pain that I was in. You know you've really hurt yourself when everything else fades away into the background. A latent need to survive kicks-in and focussing on the pain is all that matters.

On reaching the house I was rather unceremoniously flung over an arm each of Steve and James, hoisted off the sledge, up the old wooden steps to the front door, whilst in agony the whole time. I pleaded with these guys to take me to the Hospital, a mere 800 yards further down the road and the largest and most proficient Orthopaedic Hospital in Norway (complete with Helipad and used to take arrivals off the slopes at Trysil and Lillehammer) …. but no….. 'you've only got a dead leg…. trust me….I'm your best mate' came the reply from Steve.

James managed to whack my leg on the door frame as we went through, 'for Christ's sake' came my reply and at which point Mel chirped up, 'watch what you're saying Greg, you've only banged your leg'. It was fair to say nobody appreciated how much pain I was in and, having broken many bones on previous occasions, I was pretty convinced I had a fracture judging by the pain level.

I was equally unceremoniously dumped on one of the sofas and was brought a couple of Paracetamol and glass of water, 'here you go' said Ellen, a trainee Nurse at the time, 'this should sort you out once they've kicked in'.

But, despite this caring thought from Ellen I knew that it wouldn't….and it didn't. I lay there in agony wincing and almost crying. Needless to say, the party continued in the kitchen and dining area as the evening meal was prepared. The alcohol started flowing again…..but I declined. I needed a hospital and I was certain about that. Dinner was served and all the guests piled in to sit down at the dining table……but not I. I remained in agony on the sofa. 'Here McAttack, I've brought you some dinner', which he left on the coffee table along with some cutlery. But I wasn't interested.

Soon enough more alcohol had been consumed for the micky taking to kick in again. I can't think of anything worse that being mocked when you're in agony but everyone joined in, 'oh didums....is Geggy's leggy still hurting' followed by bouts of laughter, 'do you want nurse Ellen to come and rub it better' came another blast followed by, 'let me go and fetch the baby-oil' from Steve as the room fell about themselves laughing. Unfortunately, it was all lost on me.

After dinner the hoard came and crashed out on the 2 large white Sofas that Steve and Ellen had. By now we had been home for maybe 2hrs and the pain had gotten worse.

The unwanted banter continued, 'does Geggy want me to come and give him cuddle-wuddle's to make him feel better', followed by more bouts of laughter. However, Mel was now starting to realise that it wasn't an act, 'is it that bad' she spoke softly so as others could not hear? My reply was rather louder, 'yes it's bloody that bad! I'm in agony and all you lot can do is take the complete **** out of me'. My little outburst caused great delight and Steve and James nearly spat their wine out in unison!

It was now pushing toward 8pm and I'd had enough. The pain was worse and I was groaning continually. 'OK' said Steve, 'maybe we had better take him to the Hospital after all'. This was music to my ears but inside I was still angry that nobody had believed me and I'd had to wait nearly 3hrs. Either that or the evening dinner and more beverages were more important.

Ellen hadn't been drinking alcohol, so she offered to drive me the short distance to the Hospital. Mel and Steve said that they would come with me for company. I was in so much pain by now that I couldn't reach down to get my boot on, so I just left it and Steve and James carried me to the car. The car was a small Hyundi sports car.....not exactly ideal as it was so low to the ground. After further squeals of pain, I was dumped into the passenger seat. Steve and Mel walked the short distance to the Hospital by foot. On reaching the Hospital Steve had located a wheelchair, which made things easier in terms of transferring me from the car to the A&E department.

The Hospital was quiet and I was hopeful that I might be seen by a doctor quickly. Steve and Mel checked me in, which didn't take long as they had taken my passport and, like most Norwegians, the lady on reception spoke fluent English. Interestingly Norway has a reciprocal agreement with the UK on dealing with Hospital treatment, so I was dealt with as if it were our own NHS. Ellen had driven home and said she would wait to hear when she needed to collect me back. There was no point in 3 of them waiting with me and bedsides, they had other guests – James, Paula and Alexander.

So, the 3 of us sat there in silence for maybe 20 minutes, Mel on my right and Steve on my left, although Steve was incredibly giddy, still under the influence of the evenings drinking session. 'Shall I rub it for you' said Steve laughing to himself, 'No....I bloody well don't', cue more laughing from Steve.

And then, in an instant, everything changed. A door adjacent to where we were sat opened and out walked a vision of beauty. A lady, with long flowing curled brown hair, maybe in her early 30's, dressed in a white coat and Stethoscope draped around her neck. She was fabulously good looking and had half-moon spectacles. Having been slumped in his chair rather bored, Steve quickly came to his senses, his radar sprung into life and he attained a full lock-on. 'Sweet Jesus mother of Mary' Steve was heard to mutter under his breath as she drew nearer. Even Mel sat bolt upright to oversee the proceedings from here on in!

'Good evening' said the lady, 'are you Greg'……my knees were trembling at this vision of beauty…..my pain almost gone from my mind…'yes…that's right…I'm Greg'. A warm smile came my way as the lady in question spoke calmly as she leered over her half-moon spectacles, 'well…I am Anna and I am your Doctor for the evening and shall be looking after you'……… 'Hells bells…. muttered Steve again under his breath!!'. If you would like to come with me, I shall take good care of you. 'Excuse me…. I'm his girlfriend' came a sharp blast from Mel, resulting in Steve and myself swiftly turning to look at Mel, who had clearly been irked by the keen interest in the Norwegian Health Care system all of a sudden. 'And….and I'm his best mate…. I'm Steven' came a rather pathetic and unexpected cry from my chum, a less than subtle attempt to ensure he could come along and continue to drool. Mel and myself turned to face Steve in disbelief; if looks could kill. The full bloody Sunday name too…..Steven…… knew that one was coming out at some point! 'Well then' said the siren before us, 'best matey…', now drawing closer to Steve and leaning over Steve who was now all in a quiver, '…. maybe you had better come along too', she said playing him big time. Steve looked like he was going to crumble as he swallowed hard and he responded almost in a trance like state, 'erm….yes, yes doctor….I think you're right…..I think I should come along'. The steamy encounter continued…. 'well, we wouldn't want to leave YOU out would we….'. Mel and myself continued to wince and cringe, 'that's right…..I think I should be there for him' came Steve's reply, now gulping. But I had to give it to Dr Anna, she'd obviously met chancers like the one with us many times before. She had him sized up sure enough!

The bloody swine, I thought. He's been taking the proverbial out of me all afternoon and now, because I've been assigned the most attractive Doctor in Norway, he's my best mate.
'Come on then everyone' said Anna, come and follow me…. perhaps you can push the wheelchair Mr Steven'……'Oh yes Doctor, anything you say Doctor, always happy to help out a friend' came his reply. 'You lying little git' I said to Steve leaning over the side of the wheelchair so that only he could hear me. 'What do you mean' said Steve whispering into my ear, faking his surprise, 'you know I'd take good care of you if hurt or injured…. like a best mate should'. 'Right. Nothing to do with Dr Anna then, eh? You left me on that bloody sofa for hours whist you lot filled your boots!' I shot back at him.

We were interrupted as Mel gate-crashed our private conversation, 'bloody good job I'm here to keep an eye on you two….that's all I can say!' came the retort from Mel. Steve and I looked at each other and back at Mel as if butter wouldn't melt!

And so it was, off we went after Dr Anna who led us down a few corridors leading to an X-Ray Room, where Mel and Steve were asked to wait outside. She had made the decision to just crack on and get the X-ray done. Dr Anna stayed with me and along with other staff in the X-Ray room carefully helped me onto a table.

I was seen to in no time and, after being helped back onto the wheelchair, Dr Anna wheeled me back into the corridor where Mel and Steve were patiently waiting. Steve still behaving giddily. 'Follow me' said our beautiful doctor, 'I will now examine Greg's leg in another room down here, you can both come along'. When we entered said room it turned out to be an Operating Theatre, 'OH COOL' said Steve, 'an Operating Theatre!' like a kid in a sweet shop. Great, just what I didn't need, Steve let loose in an Operating Theatre when I wasn't in a position to move!

Dr Anna and Steve helped me from the wheelchair onto the operating table no-less. 'OK Greg, when did this all happen', 'about 4hours ago I replied, 'Oh….you have had to come a long way then?', 'no……not really……I'm stopping at Steve's house at the end of the street'. 'Ah….I see….well why did you wait so long as you are clearly in a lot of pain Greg' asked the doctor? 'Well…. Steve said it was just a dead-leg and they wanted to have dinner….and a couple of drinks', I replied, cursing Steve under by breath. 'Oh. I see. Is your *best mate* medically qualified?' asked Dr Anna rather sarcastically….. 'erm, well I was in Her Majesty's Royal Air Force and did a comprehensive first aid course' interjected Steve. 'Oh, that is very nice' said Dr Anna sardonically.

Dr Anna felt around my leg, 'the muscle is extremely hard, certainly damaged. Are you still in much pain, I assume that you have already taken some strong pain killers?' asked the kind doctor and she continued to feel around my leg….Steve leering jealously in the background. 'I'm in excruciating pain and no, nothing strong in terms of painkillers, just a couple of paracetamol a few hours ago'.

Dr Anna, turned to face Steve and looked over her half-moon spectacles at him whilst addressing us all, 'what, your host for the weekend and Royal Air Force first aid trained *best mate* didn't even fetch you some strong painkillers….my my'. She was playing him again and it was cheering me up immensely, 'well we thought it was just a dead-leg at the time and he seemed to be coping really well…..I think it deteriorated as the evening wore on…….he did get two Paracetamol', said Steve with some conviction. So compelling…butter wouldn't melt again! So, before leaving the Operating Theatre Dr Anna made her way to a cupboard and got some tablets and water and brought them over to me, 'here Greg, take these Co-Codamol, these are strong painkillers and will help. I'll be back shortly with the scan results.

And with that Dr Anna disappeared and she was gone for quite some time, maybe 30 minutes. Unfortunately, no sooner had Dr Anna left the Operating Theatre than my best mate set to work. Mischief was abounding, rustling through cupboards and draws. Soon enough the clown was in scrubs, rubber gloves stretched onto his hands…. fortunately, he hadn't located the scalpel…. maybe such items had been removed whilst the theatre was used as a temporary examination room? 'Ah, Mr McEvoy…would you like to bend over whilst I examine you, please sir', said Steve, in a German accent, through his new found facemask, 'no you blithering idiot…..get that stuff off before you get caught and have us all thrown out of this hospital!!' I said angrily, whilst Mel sat laughing away thinking it was all highly humorous. 'Ah, I see' said Steve, 'being uncooperative, are we? We have ways and means of making you talk' as Steve came back to the operating table now with a sink plunger he'd found. 'Please god, get me out of here' I muttered, which Steve and Mel found highly amusing'. It was like Mr Bean let loose. Steve continued to riffle through draws holding up weird and unfamiliar artefacts, with bouts of laughter from Mel.

Unbelievably after half an hour larking around he hadn't been caught in the act and started to put things back in the cupboards and took off the scrubs. I'd been stressing the whole time. I didn't need a showdown with the medical team because of this idiot.

No sooner had Steve put the last items away and the door swung open and in walked Dr Anna with a set of scans in her hand. She winked at me and spoke softly so as only Mel and myself could hear, 'it's ok, no break'. She then turned to Steve, 'well, Mr Steven....you need to be taking much more care of your *best matey'*, she said shaking her head as if in disapproval. Steve's giddiness had now gone, 'Is it bad doctor' asked Steve sheepishly, 'Oh yes. I fear the worst for this leg. I'm not sure it will ever be right....if only he had been brought in sooner'. Steve looked apologetically towards me, 'blimey mate', 'don't worry Steve, you did what you thought was best in the circumstances, you have other guests over too', I said in a sad manner. Silence fell over the room. Dr Anna had played him big time. Then she smiled, 'No break. But he has internal bleeding on the thigh. Plenty of rest, regular painkillers and I'm afraid no skiing for you on the rest of this trip'.

Steve breathed a sigh of relief, 'ah that's great, phew....and not to worry about the skiing.....he's no good at it anyway' followed by a burst of laughing from Mel, Dr Anna and Steve. Cheeky git......but I even mustered a smile myself.

We thanked Dr Anna, she'd been a great sport and dealt with things swiftly, but if I'd have been a betting man, I'd have put one on Steve's parting words... 'thanks Dr, we're only at the end of the road if you're ever in need of a Royal Air Force trained First Aider'. *Please.....someone get him out of here quickly* ran through my brain. And with that we left the hospital, where Ellen was already waiting with the car having assumed we wouldn't be much longer and decided to drive up. 'How is it, how did it go' asked Ellen, 'internal bleeding on the thigh, no skiing for me' I replied. 'Oh no! I'm really sorry to hear that Greg', said Ellen, 'I take it the medical staff looked after you well in there'. Steve smiled, 'Oh yes, the operating consultant was top drawer'. Mel shook her head, 'I think I need to share some details with you Ellen once we get back to yours!'. And with that I was once again loaded into the car and driven the short distance home where there was a little more sympathy from all than there had been earlier in the day. The strong painkillers had kicked-in and I was able to relax and enjoy the rest of the evening.

Unfortunately, for me the rest of the trip was a frustration. The next day the whole group headed off to Trysil Ski Resort for some fun on the slopes. But yours truly sat at the bottom watching and filming on a video camera the others exploits. But….all the same……..we had a tale to tell….and we had met one of the most beautiful doctors in Norway…….if not the world!!

CHAPTER 14 – TRUST ME...
I'M YOUR BEST MAN
Ian Van Dahl – Castles in the Sky

These memoirs would be incomplete if we didn't take time to recount the epic long weekend in Norway in July 2001 when Steve and Ellen tied the knot. To be truthful there were so many stories in that one weekend you could quite easily write several chapters. However, I will pull out the highlights in what was one of the most memorable weekends in my life.

Steve had proposed to Ellen at the top of the Empire States Building in New York a year or so earlier and the wedding plans were in full swing over a long period. The wedding was to be held in Norway so there was a lot of planning in terms of who and how many would be in the English Contingent travelling over and the logistics in terms of where people would sleep and how they might get to and from the wedding etc. It took a serious amount of planning. Elverum is a relatively small town and the limited Accommodation is expensive. So, plans were made for people to stay at Steve and Ellen's House and nearby log cabins and also with local family friends.

It was no surprise when Steve asked me to be his best man, it was something we'd discussed on more than one occasion when we were much younger, a pact of sorts, that we would be best men for one another. Nonetheless, it is always an honour to be asked. It makes you feel special. Having been asked, the first thing you think about is your speech.....even if the wedding is a year away, it's something that you start to think about straight-away and also about the Stag do......what can we do to him, what could we get away with? However, because Steve was living in Norway, he'd decided that he'd have a bit of a drinking session with the family over in Norway a couple of days before the wedding rather than something in the UK. And so it would be that the English contingent would travel over 3 days before the wedding to relax and have a Stag do of sorts in the sun.

It was understandable that Steve didn't come back to the UK for a Stag party as everything is exceptionally expensive in Norway and all Steve and Ellen's hard-earned cash was going into their special day. Arranging a Stag party in the UK wasn't really going to work and besides with all Steve's former RAF friends and DJ pals scattering the globe it would have been difficult to sort.

On the subject of being asked to be the best man I had the added complexity of the audience being nearly exclusively Norwegian. What was I to do? Would they all speak English and understand? Would they understand my humour and jokes? Should I learn some Norwegian? I decided that I should write my speech in English and then translate it online into Norwegian, and then teach myself. Writing the speech would be easy.....learning it in Norwegian filled me with dread!

Nearly a year later and July 2001 arrived! Steve's family and friends arranged to rendezvous at Manchester Airport, around 12 of us. Everyone was extremely excited and we'd heard that the weather was blisteringly hot in Norway. We flew from Manchester Airport to Gardermoen, Oslo's main Airport north of the city where we all caught the bus to Elverum. There was an air of excitement and we weren't to be disappointed with the weather. It was absolutely scorching!

We arrived in Elverum and several of us were taken down to the River Glomma where there was a small Campsite that had several log cabins, that Steve had rented for family and friends. Ideal and a fraction of the cost of staying in the main hotel in the town centre.

A recollection from that weekend was how much running around and hosting Steve and Ellen did. It must have been exhausting. There were the English contingent, Norwegian friends and family starting to arrive and even a number of DJ's whom Steve knew and had worked with in various Clubs around the country. Their house was completely manic and constantly full of people, his Nan, Mum and Dad stopping there, with the rest of us down by the river. In addition to all the hosting and making meals for everyone there was all the usual running around sorting flowers, bridesmaid dresses, photographer, cars etc. I didn't envy Steve or Ellen but they'd planned it perfectly and it all went without a hitch.

Having had an enjoyable first night, our first full day, and two days before the wedding, was designated as a BBQ and fun day down by the River Glomma with all the friends and family. Steve had picked an absolutely perfect location with a large log cabin that was available to hire, which had a kitchen, toilet facilities and an enormous outside BBQ. It also had free use of canoes and Kayaks. The scenery there is beautiful. The Glomma is a wide-open river with twists and turns but also has a nice shoreline along the trees. With the sun blazing down and the BBQ and beer flowing we had a truly amazing day.

Next to the river was a particularly deep pool of water with a steep embankment. I have memories of just about everybody jumping off the embankment into the pool. It was fantastic fun and massively refreshing given the temperatures. Many of the family and friends went fishing and caught Grayling, which Steve gutted and cooked on the BBQ.

After much eating, drinking and swimming I decided to give the two-man Indian canoe a go. Steve's dad, Bill, had already been out on the river with Neil, Steve's brother. Neil had decided he'd had enough and so I jumped in with Bill and we pushed off paddling towards the centre of the river. Only a short distance from the shore I became aware that there was water on the seating and it was really warm. 'Hey, Bill, it doesn't half get warm the river water over here. Have you felt it…blimey…it's so nice'? Then my world was turned upside down, 'that's not river water Greg, sorry mate but I couldn't hold on any longer…all that beer we've had'. 'You have got to be kidding Bill! I'm sat in your urine?!', 'err…. yep, it won't hurt you though'. Immediately I jumped out of the canoe shouting, 'your dad's disgusting Steve…. he's peed in the flipping boat'. Everyone on the shore burst out laughing. God bless ya Bill.

In many ways this was Steve's Stag party. Ellen had held a hen party in Elverum a few weeks earlier but for Steve this was his chance to let his hair down with his family and friends. Interestingly, at the time Mel's uncle Andrew was also out in Norway DJ'ing so was able to join us for the day and indeed the wedding.

The icing on the cake for the day was a surprise for Steve that Mel and I had kept very quiet. Elverum has a small airfield with a tarmac runway just outside town where light aircraft and gliders operated from and, long before leaving the UK, we had enquired and purchased an experience glider flight for Steve.

Mid-morning, we got some of the guys together and explained that we'd like to arrange for Steve to get kidnapped, driven to the airfield blindfolded and then surprised by his flight. It worked a treat. We were pretty much packed up for the day when from somewhere a black SUV came flying into the parking area next to the log cabin and skidding to a halt. It was deliberately dramatic. Everyone stopped to look, including Steve – what was going on? Several guys, including his dad and uncles jumped on Steve and wrapped a thick black scarf around his eyes and tied rope around his hands. Steve tried to resist but it was no use. I've no idea how or who mustered the vehicle or the scarf and rope....... but it was very scary. Steve was caught completely cold and, to be blunt, was now a very worried individual!

All the family and friends bundled into other vehicles kindly brought over from Ellen's family and friends and went in hot pursuit of the black SUV now driving at pace towards the airfield. As it happens, we'd planned a slightly longer route for the vehicle Steve was in so that the family and friends would be ready and waiting on his arrival.

Once at the airfield and with a large crowd of English and Norwegian well-wishers, Steve was bundled out of the black SUV still blindfolded. It was a great moment and there was plenty of raucous laughter! Steve's hands were allowed free whilst the Norwegian Pilot of the tow aircraft put a parachute on Steve, clearly he couldn't see it but it had the desired effect, 'looks like you are going for a jump sir' I said laughing my socks off, 'no way.... you absolute bastard!' came the cry from Steve.

The crowd, stood nearby, were besides themselves with

laughter, particularly his mum Val who I can still hear now. Steve was ushered toward the glider, that he couldn't see, the instructor holding his arm, 'I hear you are called Steven. Well my friend, before we get to the aircraft there is a small drainage dyke, I need you to jump across. It's only 1foot wide. Stand there. After 1-2-3 can you jump it for me'. This was absolute pure magic. Of course, there was no drainage dyke but being blindfolded Steve didn't have a clue. The mental strain was showing on Steve's face as the whole crowd shouted, '1....2...3!!!!' and with that Steve gave it everything and jumped about 3feet, following which he removed the blindfold. Steve looked behind him. No drainage dyke, 'you lot are an absolute bunch of bastards....... not talking to any of you'. I don't think there was a dry eye. Many couldn't breathe for laughing. But at least Steve could now see that he wasn't going sky diving but instead for a ride in a glider!

The tow plane took Steve's glider aircraft up to 4,000 feet and released it. His glider gracefully soared through the hot summer air, no doubt picking up excellent thermals. The glider twisted, turned and did no less than 3 loops in quick succession, each time getting a huge 'hooray' from the watching crowd, which now included members of the flying school. Not a cloud in the sky, nothing but delirious blue, a blazing sun, friends and family.

Better than any Stag party I'd been to and a magical moment. The glider eventually descended and landed safely. Once out of the cockpit Steve was clearly seen to be beaming ear-to-ear. It was a fantastic way to end such an amazing day. Now well into the later afternoon it was time that the party returned to their various lodgings in Elverum to freshen up ready for a mass dinner that Steve and Ellens had planned to hold at their house later in the evening.

Sure enough, a couple of hours later and freshened up, everyone retuned to Steve and Ellen's house in Elverum where a series of tables had been set outside for one mass dinner...... there was no room inside for such a gathering! It was organised chaos, but went very well. Eating Alfresco on such a warm balmy evening was special. After dinner more guests arrived for drinks, some of whom had travelled from various parts of the country to be at the wedding in two days' time.

It was during the evening that I got talking to Steve's former boss, Paul, and the founder of the Entertainment Company that Steve went on to buy a few years later. We were talking privately when I explained that I was the best man and that I was aiming to deliver my speech in Norwegian.

Paul looked at me alarmingly and raised his eye brows, 'Really? I've lived here since 1971 and speak fluent Norwegian, it's a very difficult language to learn. Let me hear you deliver it'. I wasn't so sure and felt a bit embarrassed, especially with so many people about but Paul persuaded me, 'let's go upstairs in Steve's office and run through it' and so we did. I read though the 3 or 4 pages in private to Paul and then stopped. 'I'm afraid', said Paul shaking his head, 'that you are going to die on your arse my friend and then get mocked by the Norwegians behind your back. I speak the language and I have no idea what you have just said'. I was crest fallen, which Paul could see. 'Look' he said sympathetically, 'If you really want to say something in Norwegian, which by the way I think you should and applaud you for, then keep it simple. Just introduce yourself in Norwegian and they will be happy with that. They pretty much all speak English anyway, so just deliver the rest in English. That will be enough'.

It was one of the greatest pieces of advice that I'd ever received. Paul was right and I am forever indebted for his kind support. 'Here', he said passing me some words he'd written on a piece of paper pinched from Steve's printer tray, 'this is all you need to say, I'll write it for you in English and Norwegian.

It read - Good afternoon Ladies and Gentlemen. My name is Greg. I hope that you will be able to understand me: *God ettermiddag dame og herrer. Jeg heter Greg. Jeg haper du forstart meg*'. I was so happy, 'thank you so much Paul. I'll be able to sleep tonight for sure!', 'no problem pal, least I could do. You'll go down a storm, wait and see'. And with that we returned to the party and a civilised evening.

The next day was free time for friends and family whilst Steve and Ellen went into overdrive to sort the last-minute arrangements. Although for the maid of honour Gyrid, Steve and Ellen and their parents, Val, Bill, Eva and Sigurd and myself as best man, there was a church practice in the morning. The Church practice went very well and I thought that their Priest was the spitting image of Michael Schumacher! My overriding memory was one of Steve's friends coming over to check out the Church piano that he planned to play during the wedding service. Guy is a sensational pianist but until the church practice not someone I had met before. I recall Guy coming into the Church and saying to Steve, 'where is it then' with aplomb and Steve pointing to a rather forlorn looking upright piano in the corner. It looked like it hadn't been played for years.

Guy literally blew the dust off the cover and rolled his index finger down the keys, 'It'll do. Good luck. See you tomorrow' and disappeared. 'It'll do' I thought to myself.... this boy better be good!

After the church practice I helped Steve for the rest of the day running errands. Towards the back end of the day, we were getting mightily fed up and, once the last chore had been completed, we hooked up with Steve's brother Neil who had been down at the river fishing and not had the greatest of days. On getting back to Steve's house all was quiet except it looked like Bill was ready to top himself having sat the whole afternoon in the garden with the mother-in-law, 'get me out of here before I kill her', he whispered on our return. All the other women had gone wild flower picking for the wedding posy, which is a tradition in Norway. But Steve's Nan with her dodgy hip didn't want to go, so Bill had been left with her to keep her company.

Steve laughed, 'come on, lets us 4 go for a cheeky drink in town, I'm sure Nan will be fine on her own for a short while. The girls will be back soon anyway. I think we just need to chillout now before the big day tomorrow'. Steve's Nan rolled her eyes, 'yes you lot clear off and leave me. Don't worry about me'.

I turned to Steve, 'great idea pal but I'm not exactly flush' , 'me neither' said Neil, 'Nor me but screw it…let's go,' said Bill, eager to be gone! So, we cobbled together the cash we had and set off towards the Triangle Sports Bar in Elverum, one of about four Bars in the town at the time. The rest is history. We befriended umpteen Norwegians who were surprised to see 4 British Guys on a mission on a late Friday afternoon. Before we knew it our new found friends were buying us shots, there were also drinks on the house and we were in there for hours. We spent all the money we had, which was probably around £300. And so, the day before the wedding we went and got absolutely obliterated. We were so drunk we could barely stand up. Furthermore, we'd lost track of all time and hadn't seen any family members for hours. The greatest drinking session any of us had ever been on!

Completely wasted we said goodbye to our new friends and staggered the short distance to the road where Steve and Ellen lived. On drawing nearer, we could see the vague figure of Steve's Nan sat out on the veranda in the sun, still alone. No cars had returned that we could see? The girls must still be out flower picking. Because we were so drunk, I suggested we provide a march past for his Nan, which everyone thought was a belting idea and, despite our state we formed a neat 2 by 2 and marched in unison down the road towards Steve's house. We caught Nan's attention who stared back towards us in disbelief, mouth open. As we drew nearer Bill suggested we break into a German goosestep and give the Nazi Salute at the point of passing. Understandably, we thought that this was an absolutely brilliant idea. I shall, to the day I die, never forget the look on Steve's Nan's face as we goosestepped past and, right on cue, gave her the 'Sieg Heil'. To our surprise Mel, Val and Neil's partner Vicky appeared at the critical moment, Ellen having dropped them off to go elsewhere. Their jaws on the floor, Vicky covering her mouth with her hand so as not to laugh!

I think it's fair to say that the 4 of us were in the dog-house 'big time'. We thought it was hilarious but we were all 3 sheets to the wind and the women were not happy. Steve's Nan in particular was outraged and I think Bill never got forgiven for that one. But we saw the funny side, we were drunk and we've talked about it ever since. The not so funny side is that the 4 of us were scalded massively by our partners and forced to call it a night otherwise we might 'ruin the wedding' the next day.

I don't remember Ellen dropping us off at the cabin nor sleeping in the cabin. I was comatose. I woke the next morning with a cracking headache but felt a little better after a shower. Everyone down by the river were changed into their finest and various cars arrived at the allotted time to ferry us to the Church. I, however, had to meet Steve at his house as we were to be ferried to the church in Guy's black Jaguar XJS, which was gleaming. Steve was dressed ready to go, but already pacing up and down. I asked Steve for a private word in his office upstairs, the same office where Paul had advised me on the Norwegian I should use at the wedding breakfast speech. As mentioned in an earlier chapter, you have to duck in various places so as to not knock your head on the low beams. Steve was anxious to get to the church and was wondering what it was I wanted to discuss. We sat down and faced each other.

It wasn't words I had for Steve, but a keepsake for his wedding day. I gave him the gift box, which he unwrapped, inside was a Rotary Sterling Silver pocket watch and chain, that I'd had inscribed, *To Steve, on Your wedding Day – Friendship*. It took Steve by surprise and we both welled up. I stood up a tad embarrassed and in doing so whacked my head on one of the beams. That broke my sentimental embarrassment for sure and put a lump on my head.

A year later when I got married, Steve reciprocated and presented me with a pocket watch keep sake with similar wording but very much in a Norwegian style with a Stag embossed on the front. We gave each other a hug and went down stairs to be with his parents. It was another magical moment and when Steve showed his parents the watch, they too shed a tear.

If we thought it was hot the proceeding 2 days then the wedding day was an inferno. It was well into the eighties. Suited and booted and with stinking hangovers we headed for the church, where the Priest greeted us at the entrance. I wished Steve all the luck in the world....we were ready....well almost. He was clearly nervous but also hungover and the suits were making us sweat even more and Bill for one was never keen on wearing a tie and itching to lose it. 'I feel like I've got the Sahara Desert in my throat' exclaimed Bill, 'me too, come on, let's see if there is any water in the vestry' said Steve and so the 4 amigos walked down the aisle, and through a side door next to the altar.

Sure enough there was a small vestry with a sink. One after another we gulped gallons of water to quench the unbelievable dehydration, we all had.

Unbeknown to us the Priest, aka Michael Schumacher, had slipped into the vestry and we hadn't seen him. 'Ah. I see that nerves have got the better of the British this morning. Come now, drink as much as you like. It will help with the nerves that you are all sharing this beautiful morning'. It was like the scene from Four Weddings and a Funeral! Nerves.....there may have been some nerves.....but I'm pretty sure that the ridiculous amount of beer, shots and slammers consumed the evening before in the Triangle Bar might have had a lot to do with it!! Having satisfied our thirst...for now....we made our way back into the church and started to meet and greet the guests as they arrived.

Steve and Ellen's wedding was a mix of British and Norwegian and it was a day none of us shall ever forget. They tailored it to their liking and it was brilliant. In that small wooden church nestled in the heart of Elverum came together two people that clearly loved each other and united two nations as well in a beautiful ceremony. At the appropriate point in the service the Priest told the congregation that one of Steven's friends called Guy, was going to come up and play and sing a very special song for Steve and Ellen.

I'd been looking forward to this from the 'It'll do' line the day before and silence fell upon the church as Guy walked calmly to the old small church piano that had probably been stuck in the same corner for decades and barely used. And then Guy started to play. I instantly recognised *Your Song* by Elton John. Not only was his playing majestic but his voice amazing. It's fair to say that he blew me, Steve and Ellen and the entire congregation away. There is no doubt in my mind that he's probably the most able pianist that ever sat at those particular ivories! It was a truly incredible moment and many fought to hold back the tears. Steve and Ellen could only gaze at each other and cry.

A truly spine-tingling moment, the hairs on my arms stood to attention. I could see many tissues being taken out of handbags across the congregation. An unbelievable moment.

After the Service the Bride and Groom and Best Man and Maid of Honour were put through the obligatory torment of what felt like 2hrs of professional photography. It was probably only an hour.... but it seemed to go on for an eternity in the blazing sun. Having said that, the pictures are fantastic, so it was worth it in the end.

On reaching the venue for the Wedding Breakfast, which was a huge function room at the local Museum of Norway next to the River Glomma, the rest of the wedding party were already into the fizz and beer. Everyone was outside and the rushing water of the Glomma as a backdrop made it the perfect venue. Whilst everyone was enjoying themselves, I was really starting to fret! I now couldn't wait until my speech was out of the way so I could relax! In Norway the wedding breakfast lasts about 3hrs and anyone who wants to has the chance to stand up and say a few words. However, I was pleased to hear that even in Norway the Best Man gets to speak after the Father of the Bride and Groom!

My moment came….Paul, my mentor, sat near the back watching on. I held my speech proudly and delivered the opening sentence with much gusto, *'God ettermiddag dame og herrer. Jeg heter Greg. Jeg haper du forstart meg'*. I stopped and looked up at the wedding party gathered. And then came huge cheers from the Norwegians, cutlery banging on the tables, whoops and hollering. They loved it! Paul looked across and winked. He'd saved my bacon. I continued my speech in English. 'Ladies and Gentlemen. Norway has given to the United Kingdom and indeed the world some amazing people. Edvard Grieg the composer, Edvard Munch the famous artist and, Ole Gunnar Solskaer'….a huge cheer erupted…. I continued……'so, as a token of the British Peoples appreciation, in return we give you Steven….International DJ and Chef'. The place erupted even louder than before. This had landed right in the sweet spot and the Norwegians and English alike were rolling around in tears. It's safe to say that the rest of the speech went very well and, once finished I could sit back, relax and enjoy my meal and the rest of the evening!

The rest of the evening was thoroughly enjoyable but I think that Steve, Bill, Neil and myself had burnt ourselves out a little the night before and around midnight Mel and myself called it a day and headed back towards the log cabin only a short walk away.

Steve and Ellen's wedding, along with the days leading up to it will live long in the memory. A happy time, hot balmy days in another country but where the people are so friendly and certainly share the British sense of humour. Many of those days were enjoyed with friends and family no longer with us.

So, my advice is make sure you enjoy such days, live them to the full, embrace those dear to you, laugh together, as alas nothing lasts forever and one day they will be gone.

This chapter is dedicated to the memory of Bill Redman and Sigurd Husa, Steve and Ellen's fathers. God bless.

CHAPTER 15 – ARE YOU HUNGRY
The Blackout – Start The Party

Throughout the preceding chapters, you may have noted Steve's keen interest in food. Indeed, even in Chapter 1 on our very first day hanging around together, he'd practically ordered everything on the menu at the local Fish & Chip shop! And so, in this final Chapter I thought I would pay homage once again to Steve's insane behaviour when he sees a menu with two prime examples….pardon the pun! Not only does he still do it, but his ordering 'disorder' has progressively worsened over the years.

Gluttony, should you be interested, is defined in the Oxford English Dictionary as *habitual greed or excess in eating.* Now, Steve likes his food and food is his passion and he is after all a fully qualified Chef, but is he gluttonous or does he just have a really keen interest in food, which is also his passion? That is an interesting point of discussion.

However, what I do know is that in the following two escapades it is probably gluttony…..and stupidity! Some people eat to live, whilst others live to eat……….

You have Got to Be Kidding!

Only a few years ago Steve and myself went to Manchester to see a rock band called The Blackout at the Ritz music venue. I'd heard them on the radio and fancied going to watch them live. Being in the entertainment business, Steve is always up for anything like this and doesn't need asking twice. We stopped at the Crowne Plaza Hotel and gone to a restaurant called Gorilla across the road from the Ritz for a bite before the gig. We watched the show from the balcony, well away from the mosh-pit full of sweaty students, and then drinks in a few Manchester bars afterwards. We'd had a tremendous night but had fallen into the trap of harping on and on about it a little too much in front of our respective wives. 'So, when the hell are we getting to go!' had exclaimed Ellen, his wife, during one social gathering. Hmm. She had a point.

Steve and myself had also been to see other such gigs including Bon Jovi at the Manchester Arena and, on other occasions, Whitesnake, Def Leppard and Steel Panther.

I guess we'd assumed this was a *boy's thing*, going to see rock bands and sinking a few beers, but it was clear that we were running out of excuses for taking the ladies.

Several months later I'd heard that the same band, The Blackout, were returning to Manchester but this time playing at the Manchester Academy, a venue none of us had been to before. So, I told Steve I'd get the tickets and sort the hotel given his efforts last time round. Whilst the gig was on a Friday night, unfortunately Manchester United FC had a Derby match v Liverpool on the Saturday and hotel room availability was scarce. However, I managed to squeeze us in as a well-known no frills national chain hotel in a central location. Steve wasn't impressed. Steve likes expensive, exquisite hotels with fine dining, the ones where you walk in with £1,000 then walk out the next day with nothing. But it was Hobson's choice on this occasion as even the up-market hotels were booked up.....at least that's what I told him!

We had agreed to eat at home before we set-off, so Mel and myself ate our evening meal early, the children already delivered to their grandparents for the night. Steve and Ellen had done likewise. Steve kindly picked us up and we hit the M55 motorway and headed for Manchester. We found the hotel no problem and parked up in a multi-storey carpark next door. Steve was already hating the hotel before he'd stepped foot in the place, 'I leave you to sort the hotel and we end up in one of these bloody places', he said with distain, 'we're going to a sweaty student rock concert and you'll be in here a matter of hours' I fired back. 'Besides, it's had a facelift in recent years so get over it' I added. There was some further grumbling but we grabbed our overnight bags and walked over to the reception desk to check-in.

'Right. Dump the cases I say and let's head straight over to the gig as time is marching on already', I suggested which was met with agreement. Only 10 minutes later Mel and myself were down in Reception, where we found Steve going *hammer and tongue* at the reception staff for finding cigarette butts on the windowsill in his room. The moaning continued, 'bloody cigarette butts, bloody disgrace.....bloody claiming the room had been cleaned....never again McEvoy'. It went on for a while..... but I ignored the noise. Soon enough we were outside and hailed a Taxi to take us across town to nearer the Academy. On arriving it was clear we were still early. There was a huge queue forming down the outside of the venue but, being oldies and quite happy to stand at the back of the concert hall, we headed for a nearby bar instead where we indulged in several alcoholic drinks and snacks.

Soon enough it was time to get to the gig and we walked the short distance over to the main entrance. As foreseen we were happily left with space at the back of a very hot, sweaty and insanely loud concert hall. It was, without doubt, the loudest gig I've ever been to. It was a little too much for the ladies and now perhaps they realised why Steve and myself went along to such events on our own! But we stuck it out to the end despite being blown away by decibels. After the gig all of us had ringing in our ears for maybe an hour or so.

After the gig we went for a couple of drinks in a bar across the road but were advised that they were closing and could we drink up. It was nearing midnight. 'Hey listen. Anyone else hungry' said Steve predictably, 'why don't we jump in a taxi, head back up town nearer the hotel and grab something, maybe a few drinks in a bar over there?'. Mel was first to react, 'I'm not hungry to be honest but if the rest of you are wanting to grab a kebab or a burger no problem'. 'Yeah. I'm not exactly starving but a small kebab sounds good' I replied, 'Yep, me too, sounds good' said Ellen.

At this point Steve hailed down a taxi and in no time we're heading back towards the city centre. 'Just drop us off somewhere central where we can grab a bite' advised Steve to the taxi driver. The taxi in question dropped us off in China Town, where kebab and burger take-aways and such-like seemed to be in short supply. There were however a number of restaurants, although some of these were closing up and, in any event, we weren't looking for a restaurant. Or were we……?

Having marched around for a long time and having failed to find a suitable takeaway and now with very sore feet, Steve came up with an idea. 'Look. There's a late-night Chinese restaurant here. Why don't we go in here, I'll order something, you don't have to eat if you don't want to. We can chill out and have a night cap. Save us marching around any longer'.

I think the 3 of us, who the question was directed at, were less than convinced. It was late and we were tired, especially the ladies. I know Mel was now longing for her bed. But we reluctantly rolled with it. 'Go on then' I said, 'but let's not go mad eh. Just a couple of drinks too'. Steve, looked like butter wouldn't melt, 'Trust me....I'm your best mate'.......and I knew he was going to say that too!

Before long we were sat down in a very large restaurant, which was still reasonably busy given the hour. The restaurant was in an old Victorian redbrick building and I did wonder what it might have been used for in yesteryear? The ceiling was exceptionally high, with chandeliers, probably the originals from its Victorian heyday.

The waiter took our drinks order and Steve looked over the menu whilst he was gone to fetch them. The rest of us didn't bother looking at the menu given Steve said he would order something for himself and a little extra for Ellen and myself, noting that Mel didn't want anything. The waiter returned with the drinks, Mel yawning away, clearly done and ready to turn in. Steve pointed into the menu to the waiter who nodded and disappeared. We then talked amongst ourselves, about the evening, about the band and the bars we'd been to and about life in general. It was late for us old timers now, approaching 1am. But, whilst some of us were tired, we were away from home and kids on a rare night out, so it was a civilised way to end the evening. Furthermore, Steve was right. We really didn't want to be stuck in a nightclub. We just wouldn't have lasted. 'I've ordered *quite* a bit extra, so if you do fancy eating Mel just help yourself', 'Oh. Well, I might. Thanks Steve', replied Mel.

All was going well when Steve looked rather perplexingly, across to his right where the kitchens were located, as no less than 4 waiters with 2 double layered trolleys were coming towards our table. As the trolleys and accompanying waiters drew level Steve muttered out loud, 'oh bugger. I think I may have over done it'. He was right and it was ridiculous. There was every appetiser you could think of. Sesame Prawn Toast, crackers, ribs, spring rolls, chicken wings, crispy duck and pancakes, king Prawn on skewers. It went on and on. It was stupidity to the highest degree. Mel and Ellen looked shocked. I was angry.

'What the bloody hell have your ordered' I demanded, 'I hope it's just this huge starter selection!'. Steve looked sheepish, 'errm......I don't know what I've ordered'. I was confused, 'what do you mean you don't know what you've ordered? I saw you point to something in the menu when the waiter took your order'. Steve sank into his seat even lower like a scolded school boy, 'errm.....I ordered the banquet'. 'The banquet.....you mean there's more to come!? Mel didn't even want anything!', I rebuked. It was incredulous. 'Erm. Oops. Think I went overboard even by my standards', said Steve. 'Oh, sweet Jesus' mother of Mary......which banquet did you choose.....please tell me it wasn't the mother of all banquets?'.

Steve slumped further into his seat but with a wry smile, like a naughty schoolboy replied, 'I ordered the big one.....the one for £160'. There was stunned silence for maybe 5 seconds, I then broke cover 'Holy crap....we'll be eating all night'! My jaw fell open in disbelief. 'Dick head' came a retort from his wife Ellen, 'Why?' said Mel disapprovingly. All points were perfectly valid.....and Steve knew it! 'That £160 banquet was for 6 very hungry people Steve....the kind that haven't eaten for 3 bloody days', I responded. 'Sorry folks. Tuck in though'.

With no apparent choice than to save face the 4 of us ate as much starter as we could. We were full and tired and ready to go back to the hotel....but more food was inbound. Next it was the soup.....every type......Chicken and Sweetcorn, Chicken and Noodle, Hot and Sour and Wonton. We were stuffed. But our bowls were cleared and table freshened up for the main dishes. And then in a flamboyant style the 4-waiters reappeared with the 2 trolleys again. And it was beyond insanity as the platters were delivered to our table - boiled rice, fried rice, noodles, crackers, beef dishes, chicken dishes, prawn dishes Char Sui dishes and Satay dishes.

It was completely insane. Mel and Ellen were ready for walking. Then, when we thought it couldn't get any worse, sizzling platters by the dozen arrived with steak, duck, pork, vegetables. It was mental! To conceal our embarrassment Steve took several plates full of untouched food over to a group of 4 well-built lads that had walked in, 'On us guys. You want any more just shout'....they must have thought what a greedy bunch we were! It was now 1:30am in the morning, there was a sea of food untouched in front of us and none of us good breathe. We were eating just for eating's sake and to save face. It was by far the most gluttonous scene I have ever seen. Mel and Ellen were beyond speechless although Steve seemed to see the funny side. This was making Christmas Day look like a walk in the park!

We'd eaten ourselves to a complete standstill and were slumped in our chairs. There was an air of total disgust that Steve could have been so stupid. The conversation had dried up.....the scene before us was beyond words.

And then, came the daddy of them all. A scene that shall remain etched on my brain as long as I shall live. The restaurant maitre'd came walking towards our table with a huge silver restaurant Cloche serving dish.
Whilst holding it aloft with his right hand he swept aside uneaten trays of food before us and ceremoniously lowered the huge silver Cloche serving dish into the centre of the table. 'What on earth......' I muttered aloud as the four of us stared at this monstrosity delivered before us, as Steve slumped even further into his chair in disbelief, his nose now almost horizontal with the table.

The waiter placed his right hand on the Cloche's handle and then yanked it clear in a theatrical style, 'Sir. I present to you......The Sea Bass'. And there right before us, head and tail complete, was the world's largest looking Sea Bass at 1:30am, freshly cooked in lime and a hint of chilli, ready for consumption. There were no words.....but Steve eventually found some and so did the rest of us, 'You...have....GOT.....to be kidding' said Steve. 'Total dickhead' said Ellen, 'Total Muppet' said Mel, 'Total Moron' said Greg.....

No Sir, Never During My 7 Years on Property.....

The final and most recent incident concerning Steve's menu ordering disorder occurred in 2017, during a joint family holiday to Florida.

We were well into the holiday and had been having the time of our lives at the Disney Theme and Water Parks. The weather, the rides, the food and the company.....fond memories and a time we shall never forget. Our holiday package included a dinning plan, so the cost was kept to an absolute minimum in terms of eating out, but on a couple of occasions we decided to eat out as a treat and something different away from the Coronado Springs Hotel where we were staying.

Our first of two evenings out for a meal took us to Splitsville located in Disney Springs, which is a sprawling array of shops, restaurants and bars around a lake, aimed at trapping the Disney client and spending their buck there rather than elsewhere. But it is a great place and with free bus connections to the Disney Hotels it made sense to go there. Splitsville is a huge venue with a significant number of plush 10 pin bowling lanes, pool tables and live sports, where you can play and eat with table service. But it also has a dedicated restaurant area with an excellent menu.

It is a fantastic venue and my favourite place at Disney Springs. On this occasion the waiter found us the best table in the house. A huge round table in its own glass room with views up and down the strand outside, where you could gaze upon the people walking by and the bright lights of Circus Soleil at the far end.

The menus were brought to our table and drinks ordered while the two families mused over what they might like to eat.

'Well, we all like Sushi….oh man we love Sushi so much…..yes I think I'll order that for us, said Steve. 'Oh yes…we love Sushi' qualified Lucy his daughter. 'Do the McEvoy's like Sushi?' enquired Steve. 'I'm not a fish lover at all, so not for me but the others can try it. 'Ok. Well, why don't you order something you know you'll like from the menu and I'll order a bit extra Sushi and you guys can try a bit. Save you ordering something and then not liking it. How about that then?' said Steve talking to Mel and my boys Dominic and Oliver. 'Yeah. That sounds great Steve. Thanks' replied Mel. Then came the obligatory pop at yours truly for being unadventurous, the meat and two veg guru in the corner. The fact is I just don't have the palate for seafood. When I was a kid my dad co-owned a small fishing boat.

We caught everything going, Whiting, Cod, Plaice, Mackerel, Dogfish and Sole etc. The fish would get gutted and cooked not long after catching them, often on a BBQ. But I just didn't like the taste. And why spend good money ordering something you're not going to enjoy?

The waiter reappeared, 'OK, are you guys ready for me to take your order?', he asked politely. 'Yes we are' replied Steve, 'if the McEvoy's would like to go first'. 'Thanks Steve' I said now looking at my menu to remind myself, 'can we have two Peperoni Pizza's for my boys, my wife will have the Carbonara and I'll have the Teriyaki Chicken please'. 'That's great. Thank you Sir, great choices there' said the waiter…..you've got to love American hospitality, always warm and personal. 'And your family sir', he said now turning to Steve, 'Agh, yes. We all like Sushi, so we'll have the Sushi please'. The waiter looked up from his notepad, 'Ok Sir, we have 12 Sushi dishes, could you let me know which ones you would like on the menu?', assuming that Steve had erred. 'Yes, that's right, we'd like all 12. We'd like 1 of everything please', replied Steve with much gusto. The waiter was now really quite confused, 'Sir. Are you telling me that you would like to order our entire Sushi selection? If so, that is a lot of food?'.

But Steve was already there. His food ordering disorder had caved in again, malfunctions every time a menu is presented, 'Yes. They all look good and we couldn't decide, so we'll order the lot'

There was a few seconds silence. The waiter stood there incredulously, notepad in his left hand and pen in his right hand. I decided to break the silence, 'I bet you don't get asked that one too often do you.....can I have your whole Sushi selection?' The waiter turned to me and I can hear his response as if it were yesterday, 'No Sir. Never in my 7 years on property has anyone ordered the whole Sushi menu'. Eeek. Steve had no doubt done it again. Steve chuckled and Ellen shrugged her shoulders. The waiter collected in all the menus and disappeared.

The children were really tired and as we waited for our order at least a couple of them nodded off at the table. However, after 20 minutes or so the McEvoy's *normal* food order arrived. 'Pizza looks good. Hmmm. Hope ours is on its way, I'm starving', said Steve as he looked over at the dishes just delivered.

But he needn't have worried. Two waiters were in-bound with 3 or 4 large dishes of Sushi each. It was like ground-hog day from the Chinese Restaurant in Manchester's China Town.

The huge dishes of Sushi started to land on the massive round table and, as is often to be expected in America, the portions were gigantic. Plate after plate arrived. 'Oh wow' said Lucy and Sam, 'this looks amazing, nice one dad' they continued. And it did. Only problem was they'd only brought out a 3rd of the food order. The two waiters disappeared and returned with even more huge plates of Sushi and we were already running out of table space. 'Oh bugger' said Steve, 'I didn't realise the portions would be so big'. Even Ellen was surprised, 'in the UK if you order say that dish there' pointing to one of the dishes that seemed to have swan figure cut from carrot, 'it's about a 3rd of that portion'. But it was too late to mount a defence again this monumental food ordering blunder.....the waiters had disappeared and were now inbound again with the final consignment! They delivered umpteen more plates of food. The scene again was ridiculous. There was enough Sushi to feed a Sumo Team from Tokyo! 'Oh, bloody hell....I've done it again' said Steve, slumping into his chair. 'You really are a muppet Redman', came my response. Of course, there was so much Sushi food that the McEvoy contingent who wanted to participate in trying it were able to do so. Indeed, they were able to sample every dish that took their fancy. Dominic and Mel discovered that they quite liked some of the dishes. At the end of the meal some portions hadn't been eaten. However, the Splitsville staff kindly boxed it up and the Redman's were able to eat Sushi in their hotel room for the next 3 days....! But every cloud has a silver lining and, judging by his reaction, the waiter was more than impressed with his tip for the evening, 'Sir, you can come and eat Sushi all night long whenever you want. Thank you SO much'. 'You're more than welcome. Had you working hard this evening didn't we' replied Steve.

I seem to recall Steve telling me on the way back to the hotel that it was the biggest tip he'd ever given a waiter!

And finally, my advice is, perchance you ever go for dinner with Steve and you want to avoid looking like Mr Creosote from Monty Python's *The Meaning of Life*, then tell him that the meal is on you. And whatever you do, DO NOT let him get his hands on the bloody menu!!!

CHAPTER 16 – GONE DUTCH
BONUS CHAPTER
Armand Van Helden – I Want Your Soul

The boy wonder had decided some time prior to his 50th birthday that there would be a series of events to mark this special occasion. These events were scheduled to take place before, on and after the day in question, that day being the 5th October. All of the events were of course to be extravagant and included a pals trip abroad, a dinner party for friends and family, dinner and hotel accommodation for four at a Michelin star restaurant near Blackburn, followed by a trip to Las Vegas with his wife Ellen. Good job he was only going to be 50 the once!

Some 10 months prior to the package of birthday events commencing, Steve had triggered the idea of the 2 of us going away for a relaxing boys trip and had already sought counsel and OK'd the trip with our respective wives. Good man! After a few late nights weighing up the options Steve called me to discuss. 'Good evening stumpy, Redders here. Right, I've had a look at what we could do for our relaxing, chilled out and classy weekend and here is the shortlist.......a) the Amalfi Coast, b) Cannes, c) Corsica, or d) Brittany. I've found a few good Chateaux Spar Hotels in those locations. Should be great. Fine dining, bit of a massage, nice and civilised. Which one do you fancy? Furrowed brow time, 'hmm. Sounds expensive for a lads trip. Are you paying?' I ventured, not knowing Steve's intent. 'Am I chuff', came the blunt retort...... 'typical, tight arse strikes again', came the unsympathetic response. I protested, 'hang on... I've got the eldest at University and a big family holiday planned for next year. I'm up for it, just don't want to spend stupid money'. Steve saw reason, 'OK, ok squeaky pants. I'll have another look at what we could do. Do you want me to just sort something closer to home and a little less costly?' ventured Steve. Of course this made more sense to me, 'yeah, stopping in a Chateaux might be ok with the misses but two blokes? We'd be bored pal and I'd have to pay double for the body massage! Have a look at maybe a city break, somewhere where there is more for us to do'. Steve agreed, 'yeah. No sweat.

Are you happy for me to just crack on and sort it, then tell you what we're doing?', 'yes, of course. I'm smashed out with work and my dad's not in great shape at the moment, so I need to spend time with him. Just crack on Steve and let me know where, when and how much. Just don't go mad on the price'. 'Trust me, I'm your best mate', came Steve's reply. Hmm....heard that one before. We said farewell and ended the call.
I pondered as to where Steve might take us? Maybe Copenhagen or Madrid, as these were places we'd previously discussed. Who knew? Did I trust him? Did I heck!

A few weeks later Steve called me late on a Wednesday evening, 'righty-O McAttack, everything is booked for our cultural weekend. Would you like to know where we are going? 'Yep, go on then, where to my old mucker', I said exuberantly. 'Well, we're going to Amsterdam.....and I've got a full itinerary lined up that you are going to love! All booked, just need £600 for accommodation and flights. Pay me when you want' said Steve with great delight. Cue silence. 'Amsterdam!' I blared, 'Oh no. Not doing Amsterdam with you! It's full of hookers and drugs and I ain't doing all that again....you had me in a house of ill repute back in 1991. Never again!'. Steve laughed, 'Oh diddum's.....is one worried about getting stripped naked and paraded around a seedy nightclub' he said sniggering. He continued, 'look, despite what folk think I'm NOT into all that myself. It really doesn't interest me anymore. Just trust me on this one, I've lined up some cultural things for us to do. It will be great'. I wasn't totally convinced, and reinforced my point, 'I am not going to some S&M club.......I just don't trust you in that environment. I've heard all about that space cake too. Makes people ill. Not doing it' I said rather petulantly. 'Look', said Steve with an air of calmness, 'Amsterdam is a beautiful city. I'm serious when I say it will be chilled and cultural. You've had a hard year and so have I. I swear we won't be in the red-light district....well....we'll go for a gander but won't be going in anywhere. What say ye?'. I caved in, as usual....'Hmm. Go on then, but I'll be on the next flight home if you start dragging me into funny bars!'. Steve laughed, 'don't worry. It will be great'...and with that we ended the call and settled on destination Amsterdam.

Fast forward several months and we were into September'23 and the likely lads trip to Amsterdam was looming that would kick off the months long celebrations. A *cultural* weekend in the canal city..... what could go wrong...

Steve collected me at the unearthly hour of 3:50am. It's not a time of the day most folk see, it's eerily quiet but on a plus the roads are empty and getting to the airport and parking up is a breeze. Steve, on the other hand, is quite happy at this time of day - he's often to be found baking a cake, developing a business idea or watching TV that's bad for you like Zombie

Apocalypse, whilst eating huge amounts of chocolate and drinking red wine.

The boy is nocturnal and hence he was full of beans, 'good morning Stumpy, are we ready to rumble?', came the greeting from my enthused driver and travel companion, as his music blared out rock music disturbing the suburban peace.

We were both looking forward to the weekend massively and Steve had lined up a surprise itinerary……..which is always a major cause for concern as Steve and surprises equals hair-brain ideas. However, he had assured me on umpteen occasions that this would be a 'chilled weekend'. Once out of Blackpool and onto the M55 nearby, I ventured that the girls would be jealous and it was a shame, in some respects, that they were missing out? However….. Steve advised that he'd recently had a heated argument with the misses and thus the time out was much needed. For similar reasons my wife also thought I needed time out! And thus we agreed between us that we were the best persons to be on this trip because we were the only people that liked us! That was that settled then.

The birthday boy was full of beans and broke cover whilst still on the M55, 'I've got a bit of a surprise for our accommodation, when we get there', said Steve like an excited school boy.
I know Steve too well, he is pretty pathetic at keeping secrets. 'Where are we stopping then?', I asked nonplussed, 'you'll never guess', came the reply. I knew this wouldn't take long, 'a hotel'… 'nope'….. 'a caravan'….. 'nope'…… 'a tent'…… 'nope, you'll never guess', came the gleeful reply. Now I was starting to get worried, 'a brothel' I ventured cautiously, 'nope….you don't like legs!'……..then it came to me, given the water canal

system in Amsterdam, 'a boat....my final guess'. Steve looked busted but at least we didn't have to drag the game out all the way down the M61, 'Yep! We're staying on a boat in a marina'! Whell hells bells, that actually sounded like fun and so it would prove to be.

Manchester Airport was its delightful self, rammed to the gunnels in an outdated building. It doesn't seem to have changed much in the last 35 years, despite the significant rise in travel. Roll-on the long-awaited improvement transformation programme! Steve's all singing all dancing Priority Business Lounge card didn't work either to alleviate things, there being a minimum waiting time of 30 minutes before such card holders might be allowed in. Hmmm......not sure Steve was too impressed.

Despite it being busy and slumming it with the masses, there were no flight delays and indeed our EasyJet Captain got us away 15 minutes early for the short flight to Holland. I had not been to Holland before but had an image in my mind, a place that was flat, below sea level in places, full of Windmills, Tulips, Clogs and incredibly tall good-looking people that were going to make me feel like a Borrower! All of this proved to be correct. However, I hadn't appreciated just how vast the canal system is in Amsterdam, which at just over 100 kilometres means the city almost takes on a feel not too dissimilar to Venice!

On arrival at Schiphol Airport, it struck me that the *likely lads* were now more the *likely duffers* and the trip was going to be akin to a Saga holiday. Yours truly was in agony with arthritis in the right knee and popping co-codamol like sweets and hobbling everywhere. In addition, despite numerous signs clearly articulating where the train station was [well it was clear once pointed out to us by a kindly shop assistant] the last of the summer wine possie walked for 800 yards in the wrong direction before seeking help.

Once at the station and having located a ticket machine we worked out together that the big button saying 'I want to go to Amsterdam Central' was a winner and made it easy for the old timers, as before we knew it we were on the short 25minute train ride to the Capital City.

On arrival we studied the instructions to get to the Marina where our boat accommodation was located. These advised that it was within sight and walking distance and behind the huge white building once you leave the station on the left. Despite this, duffers R Us managed to exit the station to the right and had to seek counsel from a tourist barge Captain who was stood waiting for his boat to fill with punters! It was a balmy 25degrees and trudging around in the heat the wrong way was disappointing.

Having re-traced our steps we embarrassingly found the small Marina no more than 500-600 yards away from the Station behind a huge white building, which turned out to be *Netherlands Commercial Courts* no less!

At last we reached City Marina IJDock. Tired and hot we soon perked up on seeing our digs for the weekend, the wonderful Amelia. It is a beautiful boat that sleeps 4 people, complete with 2 double beds, lounge, bathroom and 2 deck areas. We loved it, from the moment we arrived to the moment we left. Other boats passing out of the Marina created a little bit of wake, that made the boat rock gently. It was like getting lullabied to sleep. Amazing. It certainly made for an adventure. We were also extremely central, so had good access to all the best things the city had to offer.

Having taken the prime berth at the rear of the boat, Steve went down the hatch, literally, into his berth down below. Whilst he didn't have a 'normal' window view like myself, he did have a glass hatch and periodically he'd pop his head up out of it. Whack a mole indeed!

Having unpacked and found our bearings on the boat it was time to explore. We exited the marina and found ourselves on a cobbled street with a café across the road. 'Are you hungry' came the inevitable cry and before you knew it we were in a Bagel Café for breakfast.

The older duffers filled their boots but not before yours truly had spilt his morning coffee down his fresh on white T-shirt. 'Can't take you anywhere can we', came the sympathetic input.

Just before leaving the boat we'd agreed that some provisions were needed for the galley. You know, the really essential ones when you're on holiday without the misses. Beer, wine, crisps and chocolate.....oh, and some fresh orange too for breakfast. So having left the Café we put our faith in Google Maps and headed for the nearest supermarket, which was called Ekoplaza Foodmarqt.

On the way to the supermarket we clocked a bar to stop at on the way back and took in our surroundings. The network of canals is truly impressive with beautiful ancient buildings lining the banks. It became apparent to the old duffers that central Amsterdam is a dangerous place. First of all everyone rides a bike and with it being flat who can blame them. But the Dutch also have dedicated cycle roads along with a tram system.

So it felt like a never ending and complicated game of dodge like the video game Frogger, as Statler and Waldorf swerved cars, cyclists, trams, whilst vying for what little space was left with copious amounts of Tourists. The canal systems themselves were full to bursting and the tourist barge Captains certainly had their work cut out to avoid any incidents!

Finally we reached the supermarket……..and we were rather disappointed. It had a pathetic choice of our essentials and it took Steve some convincing that Hellas beer is normal lager. We left having spent a small fortune on a limited and unfamiliar choice of products. Enroute though we made good use of that café bar we'd clocked and sat in the blazing sun having a local Hoogendam beer. Steve waxed lyrical about always going for food and drink you can't get back home and how ill he thought of folk that head straight for the nearest pub that serves an English Sunday roast when abroad. 'One should always try the local food and drink' remarked my companion wisely. The Hoogendam was ice-cold and a very strong Weiss beer. It hit the mark. On returning to the boat we decided to get our heads down before heading out for dinner at a Michelin Star Japanese Restaurant selected by the food guru himself. Hmm….not so Dutch!

Three hours later it was time to get up, get showered and grab a cab to Sazanka Japanese Restaurant located across town in a 5 Star Hotel. On arrival in our Uber, I clocked a black Lamborghini getting the valet service – I was sure glad I wasn't picking up this tab! The Restaurant was upmarket. It is a Teppanyaki Restaurant, which are the hot plates that the Chef's cook the food on in front of you. Teppan means iron plate and yaki means grilled or griddled. So Teppanyaki is food that's cooked on a hot plate, it's a traditional Japanese method of cooking that produces some very tasty dishes.

Our waitress for the evening was Akiko, who introduced us to our Chef for the evening called Takuma. He was young but superb and undergone years of training in this method of cooking. He cooked us an amazing meal of Monk Fish, Sea Bass, Lobster, Wagyu Beef and Pancakes. He also spoke reasonable English. Out of politeness I asked Takuma whereabouts in Japan he came from? I could see Steve thinking *why on earth is stumpy raising this, he has absolutely no idea about Japan*? 'I come from an area called Aso' said our fabulous Chef.

He continued, 'Aso is a big area..... with a mountain, Aso is very nice'. 'That's fantastic' I replied enthusiastically, 'Steve's always wanted to go to Japan, maybe he can visit Aso whilst he's there?' I ventured. 'Oh yes, if Steve comes to Japan he must go to Aso' Steve gulped his water and, for some reason was struggling to compose himself.....again!

The meal was fantastic and, as the night wore on, other Dutch Customers joined us at the Teppanyaki, where the chatter and Japanese rice wine was flowing. As the Lobster was about to be served I asked Steve what the small reddish piece was that had been cooked separately? Steve added, 'It's the Pancreas, it's a delicacy', 'Ok...good lord......I've never eaten a Lobsters Pancreas before'........I added nervously, whilst checking I still had a suitable quantity of wine and water to wash back this little nasty coming my way.

So far during the evening I'd done pretty well with the chopsticks, but all was about to go pear-shaped. As I raised the Pancreas to my mouth for some reason my chopsticks must have twisted and I let out a cry.... 'WHOOPS.....ITS GONE!!', I'd heard that same cry in the famous World War II film *The Dam Busters*. My Pancreas shot off like a Barnes Wallis Bouncing Bomb! The much sought after piece of Lobster shot off across the room akin to the slippery little sucker Julia Roberts had to deal with in the 90's film Pretty Woman. It literally flew across the restaurant. Both Steve and the Dutch lady to his right were in pieces and literally couldn't breathe for laughing. The other Restaurant guests looked over to see what all the fuss was about. A good 5 minutes later Steve was almost composed. I on the other hand was rather sorry that the morsel hadn't managed to make its way to my cake hole. I did say cake hole there....

As the evening was drawing to a close something very peculiar happened. The lights dimmed and the whole restaurant started singing a song, which became apparent was a birthday celebration akin to singing happy birthing in the UK. Judging by the Dutch participation this was a Dutch song rather than Japanese, but the Japanese were giving it boots too as an extended entourage of Managers, Maître d' and waitresses descended on our space with a cake and candles whilst all singing and clapping. *How nice* I thought to myself that they had noted it was Steve's 50th.

But hang-on......the cake was put down in front of myself as the lovely Dutch ladies sat adjacent smiled and clapped away. I swiftly pushed the cake towards my partner in crime so as to correct the mistake, which brought a look of shock, disgust, furrowed brows a look of bewilderment and slowed clapping from my unexpected audience. Steve quickly leant over and whispered in my ear , 'I told them that it was YOUR birthday' as he slid the plate bearing cake and candles back towards myself. I smiled graciously wondering why the muppet had done such a stupid thing but at least my Dutch brethren started smiling and clapping faster having seen that I had settled for my surprise. I thus blew out my 52nd birthday candles three months early and made a wish that the muppet sat next to me would behave himself for at least a further 48hours.

We left the restaurant full and happy having had a great evening for which I was and am extremely thankful. Steve was right too, why head for an English Sunday Roast when you can have a traditional Japanese on a Friday night!

On returning to the Boat we decided to sit top deck in the warm September night air and sink a couple of beers. We did and we had a good time. But it transpired that all the merchandise from Ekomarqt tasted dreadful!

The beer, the wine, the crisps…..terrible. 'Hang-on Steve, it says here that these are *Bio* crisps', 'the bloody wines *bio* wine too!'. The penny dropped the not-so Eco warriors had been to an Eco Supermarket that sold only Eco food. Not for us.

The next morning the likely lads set off for the Heineken Experience at the old brewery, but not before we'd had breakfast. We found a trendy looking café that served traditional Dutch Breakfasts. The dynamic duo both opted for a folded type of pastry filled with sausage, cheese and garlic tomatoes. Bugger lugs also ordered a quiche, which he couldn't eat. All washed down with fresh orange and all for a very trendy 52 Euros!

We then grabbed a taxi over to the Heineken Experience. I'm

not going to fill the pages here with what that was like, suffice to say it was great and included a Heineken barge cruise after the tour.

If perchance you go to Amsterdam go and visit the old brewery. There might even be a beer with your name on it, as I found!

After a long day in the sun and a good stroll around the Van Gough museum parkland area we decided to head back for our late afternoon siesta. Come evening we were off again to a very Trendy Restaurant across the water way called Helling 7, the deal being this time I'd catch the bill. Squeaky bum time. Helling 7 was superb, a really hip modern Restaurant where we could look out over the water from a rather industrial spot as the sun set. After a monstrous Tomahawk steak and a few cocktails we were done and ready for the taxi home. Even better the bill hadn't been ridiculous.

Day 3 in the big brother boat was D-day......the other side of Amsterdam was to be exposed....the Red-Light District and all that it had to offer. However, before we got to the evenings antics, we had some real culture to take in of the approved variety.

Having had a Sunday lie in we'd skipped breakfast and set off on foot for the Dutch Resistance Museum, something Steve and myself thought might be interesting as it concerned the Dutch peoples resistance to Nazi occupation during the 2nd world war. After over an hour of walking we realised that Amsterdam was rather larger than our Google Maps suggested. Hence we decided to eat before we called an Uber.

We walked past several establishments that were all considered unsuitable for one reason or another [I wasn't having lunch at the Waldorf Hotel, despite Steve's protestations!]. Eventually we stumbled upon a rather large and authentic Irish Pub and in we went. Within minutes the menu had been inspected and two Sunday Roasts ordered along with two pints of Guinness. 'Steve.......thought you didn't like folk that didn't indulge in local cuisine when abroad, you know, the type that head straight for a Sunday Roast'. Exposed I should have expected the reply, 'Well I said English Sunday Roast and this is an Irish Sunday Roast plus it's the only place we could find'. I decided that discretion was the better part of valour and sided with my bestie, 'yeh......and what is traditional Dutch cuisine anyway? We can't eat waffles all day can we!'. And maybe he had a point, either way we'd had Japanese Teppanyaki, American Tomahawk and Irish Roast....we just weren't finding those Dutch establishments!

We caught an Uber taxi to the Dutch Resistance museum where we were educated on the pretty horrendous behaviour of the Nazi's on the Dutch population and the ultimate sacrifice many made when caught working against the Third Reich. In many cases these innocent Dutch people were helping British airmen and soldiers escape back to the UK.

We also had no idea that they had suffered a famine in 1944. Tough times for those occupied nations for sure. We left the museum in a more contemplative mood and found a corner bar where we had coffee and cake, normal cake that doesn't make you fly I should add! We headed back to the boat for our now much awaited Siesta, although yours truly couldn't sleep, so I watched TV and finished off the rather dismal Eco Pinot.

And so on to the main event! We had decided to eat once we had visited the red-light district, so after a shower and shave

the dynamic duo caught yet another Huber downtown to the place much associated with Amsterdam. I was contemplative during the taxi journey. Thinking what it might be like, how seedy it might be and whether Steve might have something stupid lined up, which was probably my greatest fear?
I didn't have to wait long as the Uber came to a stop and we jumped out into a very busy street. I really had no idea what to expect, but the reality was something less than I'd anticipated.

Firstly the red-light district is really small and we learnt later in the evening from a local barman that the female mayor of the city has done her utmost do reduce the size and scale of the red-light district business.

It is literally confined to one street with a canal down the middle and maybe 200-300 metres long on each side of the canal. Secondly, it was rammed with tourists, there were even families with kids in push buggies. There were ordinary couples of all ages queuing up to watch live shows. It was strange and had a feel of folk turning up to gawp at a freak show. Yes there were a few scantily clad ladies in some windows smiling and waving, but the pavements were packed with people from all nations and backgrounds. It did not feel seedy, intimidating or erotic. I was maybe a tad disappointed!!

We made our way to a bar a street away from the red-light district and sat outside taking in the scene, watching the world go by whilst sinking a couple of beers. There was a strong smell of cannabis in the air and a few lively youngsters around. But otherwise the atmosphere was relaxed and party like. How civilised we were, maybe 30 years earlier things might have been a little different! After our drinks we made our way to the Grasshopper Restaurant where we had a fabulous meal sat outside on the terrace in the warm September air, reminiscing on our youth and contemplating whether these memoirs might be well received by others? Eventually we returned to our wonderful boat and a night cap.

Our last day in Amsterdam turned out to be a belter. After a good lie in we took our bags to the station and left them in lockers before catching a free ferry across the river where we ate handsomely at a restaurant near the ferry landing point. Steve binged on a huge number of Oysters!

We then visited the Amsterdam Lookout Tower that provided amazing views across the city and beyond to Utrecht. We then visited *This is Holland* and did the sensory ride there, which is an amazing flight ride, similar to Soaring in Disney Land Florida, that takes you across Holland and all its major attractions. A must for anyone visiting!! But alas our time ran out and soon enough we returned to collect our bags from the station and took the short trip back to the Airport where Steve promised us a slap-up meal in the Executive Lounge. But, once again, the Executive Lounge was full to the brim and not taking any newcomers for at least an hour, much to Steve's annoyance!

And the answer to this setback I hear you cry? Well, bugger lugs settled himself down in Bubbles Champagne Bar to Caviar, Lobster and copious amounts of Oysters! And yes...he ordered everything on their limited menu! As for me.....well it was a chicken select meal from a well-known burger establishment.....and I should add that I was short changed a chicken strip!

Thanks Steve for a great weekend!

The author, Greg McEvoy (pictured right) with best friend Steven Redman aboard Mts Triton in July 1994, whilst visiting Steve who was resident DJ on the cruise ship. Picture taken during emergency drill practice shortly after leaving the Greek island of Rhodes. Steve was unbelievably put in charge of evacuation Station 9! Sweet Jesus Mother of Mary!

Greg McEvoy has enjoyed a range of Project Management roles in both the Public and Private sector in the North West of England. Greg met his wife Melanie in Blackpool and has two children Dominic and Oliver. They live just outside Blackpool.

Steve Redman initially served in the Royal Air Force as a qualified chef and, after trade training at the RAF Catering College, was based at RAF Wyton in Cambridgeshire. On leaving the Royal Air Force he became the youngest Head Chef in Blackpool. Looking to get away from it all, Steve gave up his catering career and became a DJ on Cruise Ships in the Mediterranean for a few years before moving to Scandinavia working primarily in Norway as a DJ. Eventually Steve bought the Entertainments Agency that he was working for, IDEA, and built the business up considerably over the next 2 decades. Steve met his wife Ellen in Norway and has two children Sam and Lucy. After living in Norway for 15 years Steve moved back to the UK with his family and now lives in Blackpool, the home of British entertainment.

Printed in Great Britain
by Amazon